Bible Fun Stuff

FOR MIDDLE SCHOOL

Full Tilt

Wacky Games

David C Cook

transforming lives together

FULL-TILT: WACKY GAMES
Published by David C. Cook
4050 Lee Vance View
Colorado Springs, CO 80918 U.S.A

David C. Cook Distribution Canada
55 Woodslee Avenue, Paris, Ontario, Canada N3L 3E5

David C. Cook U.K., Kingsway Communications
Eastbourne, East Sussex BN23 6NT, England

David C. Cook and the graphic circle C logo
are registered trademarks of Cook Communications Ministries.

Written by Jodi Hoch
Cover Design by BMB Design
Cover Photography © Brad Armstrong Photography
Interior Design by Rebekah Lyon
Illustrations by Marilee Harrald-Pilz

Scripture quotations, unless otherwise noted, are from
THE HOLY BIBLE NEW INTERNATIONAL VERSION® (NIV)
Copyright © 1973, 1978, 1984 by International Bible Society.
Used by permission of Zondervan Publishing House. All rights reserved.

ISBN 978-1-4347-6855-1

Printed in United States
First Printing 2008

1 2 3 4 5 6 7 8 9 10

FOR MIDDLE SCHOOL

Full Tilt
Wacky Games

Table of Contents

Introduction

If you teach middle school kids, then you have grabbed the right book. *Full-Tilt: Wacky Games* is jam-packed with wacky and over-the-top games that teach God's Word to middle school kids. We know that middle schoolers are social and energetic. They seek attention and crave excitement. *Full-Tilt: Wacky Games* will get them moving and get them excited about learning and being together. In the back of this book, a Topic and Scripture Index can help you determine the perfect game for the young teen issue or Bible concept you're trying to teach. Not only are these games fun and educational, but they provide a format for young teens to learn, problem solve, encourage each other, and work as a team. Ignite your teens with a jolt of *Full-Tilt: Wacky Games!*

The Nuts and Bolts of *Full-Tilt*

Full Tilt: Wacky Games is filled with 26 games in an easy-to-follow format. Each game in this book correlates to the *Bible-in-Life* and *Echoes* Sunday school curriculum for middle school. The games can be used with or without the Sunday school curriculum and in or outside of the church classroom. On page 112 you will find a chart that links each craft to the Unit, Lesson, and Scripture of those found in the middle school *Bible-in-Life* curriculum. The **Bible Background** illuminates the Scripture reference in a modern context. Each game offers a brief explanation of the **Application** and how it ties into the Scripture reference. **Teacher Tips** provide suggestions on how to raise the level of play or what to watch for when playing the game. Each game also offers the following:

GAME STATS: The logistics of what will be needed to successfully run the game including:

Group Size: Small groups range from 2–16 players. Large groups are considered to be more than 17 players. Some games can be played using either small or large groups.

Activity Level: There are three activity levels.

Level 1 is the lowest level requiring minimal movement.

Level 2 requires a moderate amount of movement.

Level 3 is the highest level of energy. Expect the game to be fast-paced and on the wild and crazy side.

Space Needed: Almost every game requires a cleared playing area in a classroom. However, some require more space, such as a gymnasium or outdoor field.

GEAR LIST: The materials needed for the game. We've kept in mind materials that are easily accessible and quickly gathered for your convenience.

WARM UP: This includes brief instructions on how to set up the playing area or materials that need preparation beforehand.

GOAL OF THE GAME: A concise explanation of the objective of the game.

FULL TILT: Specific instructions and teacher-directed talk explaining the nuts and bolts of the game.

FINISH LINE: These three debriefing questions help students analyze the meaning of the game and apply this meaning to the Bible and their lives.

Fill Your House

Scripture Reference

Deuteronomy 6:6–9, 20–21, 24

Memory Verse

These commandments that I give you today are to be
upon your hearts. Impress them on your children.
Talk about them when you sit at home and when you walk along
the road, when you lie down and when you get up.

Deuteronomy 6:6–7

Bible Background

It is traditionally accepted that Moses wrote the Book of Deuteronomy between
about 1446 and 1406 B.C., while the people of Israel were wandering in the
wilderness prior to their entrance into Canaan. Deuteronomy is a renewal of
God's covenant with His people before they entered the Promised Land.

Society today separates church education from daily education. In fact, in most
places, trouble will begin to brew if the two are intermingled in the public sector.
But in Moses' time, the Hebrews took very seriously their role in educating their
children in the things of God. Education took on a broader and deeper meaning
than today's typical school setting, extending far beyond the basics of reading,
writing, and mathematics. The Hebrews were commanded to fill their homes with
God, and they took that command seriously.

God wants us, too, to fill our homes with Him. Because the great truths of God
go to the very heart of our being, they must be part of our total life experience.
Where we sometimes get off track is in losing sight of how God has made us into
new creations upon accepting Christ. The old has gone; the new has come! Are you
still holding on to any of that old stuff that God wants to clean out? What things
need to be tossed out of your home and heart to make more space for God? Let the
Lord take all the old junk away and fill you with Himself instead.

Teacher Tips

Use two different colored streamers to help players determine who is on which team. Tie colored streamers to the right arms of all the players on each team.

You might choose to write other things such as *friends*, *computers*, *TV, music*, etc., on the balloons instead of *God*. This will limit the number of God balloons available, and make the teams search for God balloons amongst the other things that clutter our homes.

Game Stats

- **Group size:** Small or large group
- **Activity level:** 3
- **Space needed:** Large open space

Warm Up

Inflate balloons. Write "God" on each balloon. Store the balloons in the garbage bags.

Cut the tops off the boxes. Use the masking tape to make a base line for each team. Place a box on each side of the playing area between the back line and the playing line.

Gear List

- Masking tape
- 2 very large boxes (same size)
- Thirty 10" or 12" balloons (plus a couple of extras)
- 2 large garbage bags
- Permanent marker

Application

With media, music, and computer technology, teenagers fill their homes with a whole lot more than God. This game aims to focus their thinking on the value of filling their homes and their hearts with God and God alone.

Goal of the Game

Teams will be trying to fill their box with balloons. The team that fills their box with the most balloons wins.

Full Tilt

Divide the group into two teams. Have each team sit behind their team's base line. Spread the balloons out in the middle of the tagging zone.

What fills our homes? Often we let television, music, video games, and computer chatter do that. God says in Deuteronomy to fill our homes with Him. In this game you'll get to practice filling your house with God. Point to the box, each team's "house." Point to the balloons with "God" (and possibly other words) written on them. **When I say, "Fill your house," each team will begin to pick up balloons. Team members may only pick up one balloon at a time. Here's the catch. If you're in the middle of the playing area, the tagging zone, you can be tagged by a member of the other team. If you're tagged, you have to drop your balloon. Then you have to run to your team's baseline before you can come back for another balloon.**

If you spot anyone not following the rules, take a balloon from their "house" and put it back into play. If a team pops a balloon, they'll be penalized by having two balloons added to the other team's house. The team with the most balloons at the end of the game wins.

Finish Line

- **What does it mean to you to "fill your home with God?"** *(put God first, make Him a priority, make your life more about God than about other things like TV, music, friends, etc.)*

- **When you look at the things that fill your home and your time, what would an outsider think is important to you?** *(Answers will vary.)*

- **Why does it matter whether or not you fill your home with God?** *(God wants to have a relationship with us, so we need to spend time with Him. The things we value are what we spend the most time doing and thinking about. If we're serious about knowing and following God, we will make more of an effort to have Him take up more space in our lives and other things take up less. The things we think are valuable are what we fill up our lives with, etc.)*

Treasure Hunt

Scripture Reference

Joshua 1:8; Psalms 1:2; 119:11, 15, 47, 97, 165;
1 Timothy 4:15

Memory Verse

Do not let this Book of the Law depart from your mouth;
meditate on it day and night, so that you may
be careful to do everything written in it.

Joshua 1:8

Bible Background

Moses and the Israelites had been stuck in the desert for 40 years because of their disobedience to God. In this passage, Joshua was taking over the leadership of the Israelites from Moses. Joshua would be the one to lead the Israelites into the Promised Land. God reminded Joshua that the key to the promises now being fulfilled was the people's obedience to God. To obey God's laws, the people needed to remember them, focus on them, and meditate on His words.

God commanded the Israelites to think about His commands at all times and to teach them to their children in a variety of settings. These verses from Psalms impress upon us that we're to meditate on God's Word continually—from the moment we get up in the morning to the last waking thought before sleep.

Contrary to what many think, the time we spend involved with God's Word was never meant to be limited to a devotion time once a day; God's Word should be a vital part of our daily experiences. What can you do to make God's Word ever-present in your life? How can you lead your students to experience the continual presence of God's Word in their lives? The more we devote ourselves to the Scriptures, preaching, and teaching, the more we'll grow and discover the treasures God has in store for us.

Teacher Tips

During the game, when "treasures" fall off the shovel or spill out of the boxes, the items are "out" of the game and cannot be collected and placed in the team box. You can change the rules and allow the other team to pick up any spills, if desired.

If you play outside, you can exchange the boxes for buckets and replace the various contents with water. Place an empty bucket at the start of each team line. Mark a line at the same height on each of the team buckets. The first team to fill their bucket to the line with water wins.

This game can be played by any size group, from 6 students to many. Large groups can be divided into 3 or more teams, just adjust your supplies accordingly.

Game Stats

- **Group size:** Any
- **Activity level:** 2
- **Space needed:** Classroom space or outdoors

Warm Up

Cut the newspaper into two-inch strips. Set up the playing area: put three boxes at one end of the playing area. On each box write one of the following: Joshua, Psalms, 1 Timothy. In each box put one of the following items: cotton balls, packing peanuts, newspaper strips.

Use masking tape to indicate two start lines 10 to 15 feet away from the three boxes. Place a box and a shovel behind each start line.

Gear List

- Three 3-foot deep boxes without lids, plus one per team
- 250 cotton balls
- Large quantity of packing peanuts
- One large newspaper, shredded into 2" strips
- 1 small plastic shovel per team (Alternately, use kitchen scoops or large plastic cups.)
- Marker
- Masking tape

Application

Many middle school youngsters seek "treasures" in worldly places—with friends, in music, television, and inappropriate activities. In this game, young adolescents find buried "treasures" when they dig into God's Word.

Goal of the Game

Each team will use a shovel to transfer the contents of their full boxes to their empty box. The team with the most "treasure" or items from each box wins.

Full Tilt

Divide the group into two teams. Have each team line up behind their team line. **To really know God we need to dig into His Word. In this game, you'll use the shovel to dig into the full boxes, which stand for God's Word. Then you'll bring the treasure you find back to your team. Fill up your team's box with all treasures as you can.**

Point out the boxes at the other end of the room. Explain that each box is filled with different items. At the starting signal, the first player on each team will run to one of the boxes, use the shovel to dig into the box, and return to their team with a shovelful of stuff. Once back to the team line, the player will empty the shovel into the team box, then hand the shovel to the next player who will then race for the three boxes. Items that fall off the shovel in transport or spill from the boxes cannot be picked up or used again. Continue play until all the items in the three boxes are gone. Have each team count or measure the items in their box. The team with the most treasure wins. You can also end play by calling time rather than waiting for the three treasure boxes to be emptied.

start

Finish Line

- **What kinds of treasures do you find when you dig into God's Word?** *(truth, things to help me, God speaking to me, answers, encouragement, correction, etc.)*

- **Why does God want us to dig into His Word?** *(to build our relationship with Him, to know what He says, to understand life better, etc.)*

- **Have you heard God speak to you through His Word? If so, what did you hear Him tell you?** *(how much He loves me, that He has a plan for me, that He will make a way for me, etc.)*

Hey, Obey!

Scripture Reference

1 Samuel 15:1-3, 7-15, 20-22, 24-26, 28-29

Memory Verse

If we claim to be without sin,
we deceive ourselves and the truth is not in us.
If we confess our sins, he is faithful and just
and will forgive us our sins.

1 John 1:8-9a

Bible Background

The Amalekites were bitter enemies to the nation of Israel. A warring people who made a habit of invading other nations and capturing their possessions and citizens, these warriors also worshipped false gods. They were in complete opposition to God's laws and people. In fact, they were the first group to attack the Israelites after the Jews reached Canaan, and they continued to harass God's people in an effort to destroy them. God did not want these godless people to contaminate the Jews with their idolatrous ways, so He directed King Saul to completely destroy the Amalekites.

Saul did destroy many of the Amalekites and their belongings—but not all of them. He disobeyed God's explicit instructions by keeping the best of the best of the Amalekites' goods. When God confronted Saul about his disobedience, Saul made excuses and even blamed others for what he did.

Saul trusted God for the victory when facing a battle. But once the battle was won, he no longer felt the need to obey. Saul chose not to ask for forgiveness for his sins until he had lost his position. Are you obeying God in battle and in victory? When you disobey, do you repent from your heart or are you merely regretting the painful consequences? God wants us to obey Him and not make excuses for our actions. Continue choosing to give yourself to God in each new circumstance, for your obedience is a precious gift in which He takes great delight.

Teacher Tips

Take time before the game to explain some qualities found in a good team. **Teammates work with each other and use positive words to build their teammates up. Think of a team as a large centipede with each team member as one of the legs. Each leg has to work with the others. If one leg decides to do its own thing, what happens to the centipede? On a team everyone is in the game together—a team wins together or loses together.**

Some young people will struggle with having to suffer a consequence for what a teammate does. The first time a team selects an "Excuses" envelope, someone may decide she doesn't want to play because she doesn't think it's fair to follow the "Punishment" card since she didn't select it. Point out that in team games everyone participates in the good and the bad, the easy and the not-so-easy.

Game Stats

- **Group size:** Small or large group
- **Activity level:** 1
- **Space needed:** Classroom

Warm Up

Use masking tape to mark out the following (see diagram on page 17). Mark a goal at the front of the room. You might wish to set a chair in the front of the room with a bucket of candy sitting on it. Use 2 sets of lines to indicate 5 feet, 10 feet, 15 feet, and 20 feet from the goal. Teams start 20 feet away from the goal. Depending on the size of your group, you might wish to add lines for 3 or 4 teams.

If you are using 2 groups, number the envelopes from 1–14. If you are using 3 groups, number the envelopes 1–22, and for 4 groups 1–30. Make a pile of 5 or 6 "punishment" cards. Punishments might include 15 sit-ups, 15 toe-touches, 15 jumping jacks, sing a song, spin in place 10 times, or leapfrog around the room one time.

Gear List

- Index cards (14–30 depending on group size)
- Masking tape
- Envelopes (14–30 depending on group size)
- Pencil or pen
- Chair
- Bucket of candy (optional)

Application

Middle school kids are masters at making excuses and blaming others for their actions. In this game, students learn it's best to obey God. Obeying God will be much easier and will end in success. Making excuses will create more pain and challenges and will ultimately keep them from succeeding.

Goal of the Game

Teams try to be first to reach the goal by choosing and following instructions on "Obey God" and "Excuses" cards. A team advances and/or suffers punishment as a collective group.

Full Tilt

Divide the group into teams and sit them at the line farthest from the chair. **God wants us to obey and do things His way.**

Write "Obey God" on 7 cards.

However, there are many times we find ways to convince ourselves that our way is better than God's way. We make excuses for our disobedience. What are some common excuses we might use when we know we've blown it and disobeyed?

As a group, think of seven common excuses, write each on an index card and label these cards "Excuses." Shuffle the cards, and then place each card in one of the numbered envelopes. Lay the envelopes where the teams can see them with their numbers showing.

Each team will take turns selecting an envelope. If an envelope containing an "Obey God" card is selected, your team will chant, "Hey, hey, hey, God wants us to obey and do it His way." Then your team can move forward to the next line toward the goal. If an envelope with an "Excuses" card is selected, the team does not advance. The team must then select a "Punishment" card and the whole team must complete the punishment. The first team to the goal wins. (If using 3 teams, you will need 11 "Excuses" cards and 11 "Obey God" cards. If you are using 4 teams, you will need 15 of each type of card.)

Finish Line

- **Why do you think you had to select a punishment card if you made an excuse?** *(because I wasn't taking responsibility for my actions and choice, I didn't do what I was supposed to do, I made excuses instead of obeying, etc.)*

- **Why do you think it's sometimes hard to make the decision to obey?** *(It seems like I won't get what I want. It doesn't look fun. It makes me stand out from other people my age. I don't like doing what obedience requires, etc.)*

- **Tell about a time when it was a hard choice to obey.** *(Answers will vary.)*

Cool Covenant

Scripture Reference

2 Samuel 7:8-17; Hebrews 8:10-13

Memory Verse

Christ is the mediator of a new covenant,
that those who are called may receive
the promised eternal inheritance.

Hebrews 9:15

Bible Background

Love letters are often full of promises—promises to love, to be faithful, to care for and protect the beloved. The same is true with God's love letter to us—the Bible. Since God is loving and faithful, we know that He will always be true to His promises. We can read about God's faithfulness in keeping promises to His people in one Bible story after another. We know we can trust God because of His promises to us. God loved us enough to promise to send His Son, and then to follow through. And with His Son, He established a new promise: that we can be with God forever.

Many middle school students have unfortunately experienced "broken" promises in their lives. They're left with a skewed perspective on the meaning of "promises" and may be jaded or cynical about someone claiming to always keep a promise. These young people need to realize that God's promises are different from what they've experienced in their lives so far. God makes promises that cannot be broken. He initiates and reaches out to us by giving us a promise. Then we must do our job by grabbing hold of the promise.

You have the privilege of extending this awesome promise to middle schoolers who are fearfully and wonderfully made in His image. May God's blessings be poured out on you as you accept this incredible and joyful responsibility.

Teacher Tips

Demonstrate how to gently tag people's hands using the pool noodle. Be sure to give examples of what not to do as well. Finish your demonstration by asking three students to demonstrate appropriate tagging with the noodle.

With this game some youngsters might tend to be more aggressive than others. If a teen is too aggressive, pull him aside and ask him to restate the rules for tagging other players. Explain what you've seen that is inappropriate. Ask him to show you the appropriate way to tag others. Then ask him to restate your expectations.

Game Stats

- **Group size:** Large group
- **Activity level:** 1
- **Space needed:** Large open area

Warm Up

You'll need a large open area free of obstacles.

Gear List

- 2–4 swimming pool noodles

Application

God wants us to grab hold of His promises. In this game, students will have to grab hold of God's promises and try their best not to let go. They will also have to trust that holding on to the covenant will not lead them in a way that will hurt them.

Goal of the Game

Two to four players with "covenants" (swimming pool noodles) gently sweep the pool noodle past posed players who grab on to the noodle and keep holding on as the covenant holder continues to extend the covenant to other players. The group with the most players hanging on wins!

Full Tilt

God gives us promises called "covenants" to hang on to. This noodle represents a covenant. Show the swimming pool noodle. Select two to four players, depending on the number of noodles available. Hand each of these players a noodle. **These players will be the covenant holders.** Send those players to the center of the playing area.

The remaining players should spread out around the room and strike a pose with at least one hand away from their bodies. **Here's the tricky part for you posed players: keep your eyes closed! When I shout, "Cool Covenant," the covenant holders will begin to sweep the noodles past the posed players. When you sense the covenant sweeping past you, try to grab the noodle. Once you are holding on to the noodle, open your eyes. Now you're a part of the covenant-tagging team. Be sure to hold on tight and don't let go.**

Covenant holders, you must carefully lead those following you as you try to add more players. The game is over when everyone has grabbed on to one of the covenants. The team with the most holding on to their noodle wins.

Finish Line

- **How was grabbing the pool noodle like holding on to God's promises or covenants?** *(All I had to do was hold on when it was presented to me. I had to pay attention to when it came by me. I had to work to keep holding on. It was hard to keep holding on, etc.)*

- **Why is it hard for some people to hold on to God's promises or covenants?** *(They don't see them. They don't think the promises are for them. They don't trust God or believe in God. They can't see what God is trying to do, etc.)*

- **Could you tell exactly when or how the noodle was going to come to you?** *(No, I could hear them approaching but I couldn't tell exactly. It was hard to know. I kept guessing, etc.)*

- **How did this game help you understand more about God's promises or covenants?** *(I can try harder to hold on to His promises. I can take a chance at trusting God. I won't be so quick to let go when it gets hard, etc.)*

Hang Out

Scripture Reference

1 Kings 11:1–10

Memory Verse

He who walks with the wise grows wise,
but a companion of fools suffers harm.
Proverbs 13:20

Bible Background

Solomon, one of the wisest people who ever lived, came to the end of his life a broken man. This lesson is a startling contrast to the time when Solomon asked God for "a discerning heart to govern your people and to distinguish between right and wrong" (1 Kings 3:9).

Even though he had extraordinary wisdom, Solomon learned the hard way that it matters to God who you call your companions and friends. God wants His children to hang out with people who obey Him and follow His rules. Solomon made a poor choice in the people with whom he surrounded himself. Because he wanted to gain political advantages, the wise king associated with individuals who did not honor God. Solomon ended up paying the price for his bad choices.

Who you hang out with matters to God. Without even realizing it we begin to talk, act, and even think like those with whom we keep company. Prod your middle schoolers to learn from Solomon's experience. Let them know that being alone for a short while would be better than hanging out for any length of time with the wrong crowd. People around us can influence us for good or for bad. In the same way, we can influence those around us in a positive way.

Teacher Tips

Some students who are not as social as others will have a harder time going right up to someone. Have a signal for students who need to find another student while playing the game.

For larger groups, you might need to extend the exchanging time from one minute to two minutes. You might also choose to draw more than one number from the bag for negative impacts.

Introduce the concept of "guilt by association." Talk about what types of choices people make that have a negative impact on us, even if we aren't the ones who actually made the choice.

Game Stats

- **Group size:** Any
- **Activity level:** 1
- **Space needed:** Classroom space

Warm Up

Before the game, based on the size group you have, put enough hats, bandanas or head bands in a box, enough for one-fourth to half the total number of players. Also in the box, place enough gloves, wristbands, and/or bracelets for the remaining number of players. Mix up the items.

On the same number of cards as you have headwear, write "bad influence." Write "good influence" on the same number of cards as you have arm wear. Keep these cards in your hand; you'll give a "bad" card to each student who chooses headwear, and a "good" card to each who chooses arm wear.

Gear List

- Index cards, one per player
- Pencils, one per player
- Slips of paper, one per player
- Large box or bag
- Headwear: baseball caps, knit caps, bandanas, headbands (enough for ¼ to ½ the students in your group)
- Arm wear: wristbands, bracelets, gloves (enough for the remaining number of students)

Application

Show your middle school students that it does matter who they hang out with, whether those people have a negative or a positive influence. Help them understand it matters to God, it matters to their parents, and it ultimately matters for them. In this game, students will learn how hanging out with the wrong people, even for a short time, can have an effect on them.

Goal of the Game

Players will try to figure out which other players are not good influences and seek to avoid them. The two or three with the fewest number of "bad" contacts win.

Full Tilt

Before we start, you each need to find out if you'll play the part of a "bad" influence or a good one. Only you will know what you are. Your goal is to circulate through the room, collecting people's autographs. You want to collect only the autographs of people who have a "good" influence. As you go along, you'll hopefully begin to figure out what identifies a "bad" influence so you can avoid them. At no time can you give any clue about your own or someone else's influence identity. You're playing to win by collecting just the autographs of the people with a "good" influence.

One by one, let students choose a headwear or arm wear item from the box. If they choose a headpiece, give them a "bad influence" slip. Those taking an arm piece receive a "good influence" slip.

Put on your item and put your slip of paper away, out of sight. Hand out the index cards and pencils. **As you walk around the room, you can stop and talk to anyone. Once you stop near someone, you need to hand them your card to sign, and you will sign theirs. If you're a bad influence player, your autograph is an X, so write that on each card you're given. If you're a good influence player, your autograph is an O. At no time can you sneak a peek at what someone is writing on another's card. Try to decipher who the "bad" people are and avoid them, while collecting as many O autographs as possible.** Set a time limit, say "Go," and let kids socialize. When time is up, students total their Xs. The three with the fewest Xs win.

Finish Line

- **Even though you didn't hang out directly with a bad influence, how could that person possibly affect you?** *(Possible answer: I could pick up something negative from someone who hung out with a person who has a negative influence.)*

- **Give examples of some negative and positive effects people can have on you.** *(pick up bad habits/good habits, start hanging out with a worse or better crowd, etc.)*

- **Share a choice you made that affected you in a negative way.** *(Answers will vary.)*

- **Share a choice you made that affected you in a positive way.** *(Answers will vary.)*

✳ Winner's Circle

Scripture Reference

1 Kings 16:29-31; 18:17-24, 36-40

Memory Verse

Therefore put on the full armor of God,
so that when the day of evil comes,
you may be able to stand your ground,
and after you have done everything, to stand.

Ephesians 6:13

Bible Background

When you are on God's side, you will be on the winning team. Elijah had a good grip on this fact. Most of God's prophets had been killed, and Elijah was the last remaining one. It seemed as though the odds were against him. The 450 prophets of Baal were pitted against just one of God's prophets—Elijah. The challenge seemed impossible. Humanly speaking, Elijah was doomed to be the loser.

But Elijah won the battle because he was on God's side. When Elijah called on God, God delivered the winning display of power. The 450 prophets of Baal were powerless. Your middle schoolers need to know about the God who has amazing power, who can do the impossible, and who can help them beat amazing odds. Give them the truth that they can know they're winners because they have God on their side.

In old television shows, you always knew who the good guys were and who the bad guys were. Everything was simple and clear. However, today, the lines are not as well defined. We may sometimes be uncertain about what is right and what is wrong. Our middle schoolers have the same questions. They are not always sure about what God would want them to do in certain situations.

This week take time to pray that your students will be alert and able to recognize the good and evil in their lives. Pray that they will learn that God's side is the winning side. Pray that they will learn to take a stand for God and trust that He will take care of them, no matter what the circumstances.

Teacher Tips

This game can get wild and crazy as it picks up speed. Emphasize how to safely get out of and into seats. Let students know pushing and knocking each other over will take them out of the game. Encourage them to have fun, but to be safe and remain in control.

Be sure all the players in the middle say the phrase loud enough so all can hear. Some players will have a hard time saying the phrase, because deep down they don't feel like real winners. Be sure to touch base with these players afterward, and reassure them that real winners are winners because of who God says they are, not because of what they may feel about themselves.

Game Stats

- **Group size:** Small group
- **Activity level:** 2
- **Space needed:** Classroom

Warm Up

Set chairs in a circle. Be sure middle of the circle is free of obstacles. You will need one less chair than you have players.

Gear List

■ Chairs (one less than the total number of players)

Application

Everyone will have a chance to be a winner in this game. This game is full of opportunities for the young people to scream and shout out the good news to others. We are all winners if we are on God's side.

Goal of the Game

Players will sit in a circle and listen for a defining "winning" characteristic, given by the person in the center. Players who possess this characteristic will stand up and move to a new seat. The player who doesn't move fast enough to get a new seat becomes the new person in the middle.

Full Tilt

Have everyone sit in a chair around the circle. Explain: **Elijah was a winner because he was on God's side. We are all winners when we're on God's side. The person in the middle will call out something like this: "I'm a winner on God's side. We are all winners, especially if we _____."** (Name a characteristic such as have shoes that tie, have brown hair, are wearing red, etc)

All the players around this circle with the characteristic I just called out must stand and find a new chair. The person in the middle needs to find a chair too. One player will be without a chair; this is the new "winner" who takes the center of the circle. The person in the middle begins the next round by repeating the phrase, "I'm a winner on God's side. We are all winners, especially if we _____."

Finish Line

- **How is a winner on God's side different from a winner of the world?**
  (A real winner knows that God believes in him or her, no matter what. A winner on God's side doesn't depend on what others say or what others expect to be a winner. A winner on God's side believes what God says, not what the world says, etc.)

- **If you are on God's side, why would you be considered a winner?**
  (because I trust in what is right, because I will get the best reward in the end, because no matter how it looks, I'll come out ahead in the end, because God will watch out for me, etc.)

- **How do you think God defines a winner?** *(someone who obeys, someone who trusts what He says and does what God wants, someone who follows God no matter what other people are doing, etc.)*

Clean It Out

Scripture Reference

2 Kings 17:6–8, 11b–14, 16–18, 22–23
2 Chronicles 36:11–12, 14–17a, 20

Memory Verse

Do not be deceived: God cannot be mocked.
A man reaps what he sows.

Galatians 6:7

Bible Background

Here's a basic truth: God hates sin and sin has major effects on others and us. Just take a look at the history of God's people, the nation of Israel. In this text we see Israel's fall. Not because their people weren't prepared for battle, or for any reason other than sin. Every time Israel turned from God, He sent a prophet as a messenger to tell the people to change their sinful direction. He would plead with them to reverse their ways and follow Him. When the people didn't listen, God sent punishment. Clearly, God is serious about getting rid of sin in our lives.

Which sins have the worst consequences? Can't you almost hear your middle schoolers asking this question? Most of us tend to think that the worse the sin, the more awful the results. The consequences of murdering someone should be more severe than for telling a lie, right? In earthly terms, maybe, but not in God's eyes.

Any and every sin brings the consequence of death: separation from God now and forever. That's the bad news. But there's good news too! All our sins, regardless of how we "rate" them, are forgivable. God judges our wrongs, and He also provides the way to clean the slate. We can each be justified, or declared not guilty, simply by receiving the gift of God's grace. Knowing that sin has consequences is only part of the story. The rest is that there's still a way out for those of us who stumble and fail. Only God could give us such a window of hope every day. Help your kids understand the God who judges sin is also the one who provides a way out from under it!

Teacher Tips

Be sure everyone holds the tarp with both hands at all times. Players will be very tempted to use their hands to stop balloons from falling off the tarp. If you see this happening, be sure they understand there is a consequence, and toss a black balloon back onto the tarp.

Game Stats

- **Group size:** Small or large group
- **Activity level:** 2
- **Space needed:** Classroom

Warm Up

Inflate balloons. You can easily transport the balloons by stuffing them into a large trash bag.

Gear List

- Small tarp or large blanket
- 5 black balloons
- 15 balloons of different colors
- Stopwatch
- Large trash bag if transporting balloons

Application

God wants us to get rid of all the sin in our lives. In this game, everyone works together to try to get rid of sin. Even what seems like a small amount of sin is too much and gets in the way of our close relationship with God.

Goal of the Game

Players will hold the edges of the tarp, on which are many balloons, and work together to get rid of sin represented by the black balloons.

Full Tilt

Spread the tarp or blanket on the floor. Have the players stand around the edge of the tarp or blanket and take hold of the edge with both hands. **God wants us to get rid of sin. Sin offends God and it hurts us.**

Toss the balloons onto the tarp. **These black balloons represent sin. Try to get rid of the sin by working together by raising and lowering your arms. You cannot use your hands to take balloons off the tarps.**

Time the group to see how fast they can all work together to dump the black balloons. Anytime a colored balloon falls off of the tarp, the group is penalized by having a black balloon added onto the tarp.

Each time the group plays, time them to see if they can better their time. If you have a large group, use several tarps so groups can compete against each other. The first group to get rid of all of its black balloons wins. When everyone is finished playing, pop the black balloons and have everyone shout, "God can take away our sin."

Finish Line

- **How can you get rid of sin in your life?** *(Ask God for forgiveness. Admit what I did wrong and say I'm sorry to God, etc.)*

- **What are the consequences of sin that you have seen in your life or in other people's lives?** *(People don't get along. Kids get suspended or kicked out of school. Adults lose their jobs. People get into trouble or get fined or arrested. We hurt people's feelings or lose our friends, etc.)*

- **Why do you think we ignore God's warnings or directions, like the people of Israel did?** *(We think we can get away with it. We want something too badly to care about the consequences. We get carried away and forget about the consequences. We let someone influence us, etc.)*

Books of the Bible Battle

Scripture Reference

Nehemiah 8:1–12

Memory Verse

The law of the LORD is perfect, reviving the soul.
The statutes of the LORD are trustworthy,
making wise the simple.

Psalm 19:7

Bible Background

The books of Ezra and Nehemiah tell of the rebuilding and reorganizing of the Jewish people after they had been taken to Persia as captives. Not only did the people long to be back in their homeland, they longed to be spiritually whole again. For years they had searched in all the wrong places and worshipped false Gods. Ezra and Nehemiah helped the Jews look to the Bible for their healing during this time.

In the Bible book bearing his name, Nehemiah, who led the effort to rebuild the walls around Jerusalem, gathers the Israelites together to hear the reading of God's Word. Nehemiah realized how parched for spiritual truth and comfort the Israelites had become. In the Book of Ezra, the people experience a spiritual revival after Ezra reads God's Law.

Just like the Jewish people found comfort and joy in the Scriptures, people today can do the same. In our time, people are searching in many wrong places to find belonging, love, comfort, and joy. They're hungry for the real truth of God. Where do you go when you're feeling overwhelmed and run down? What better place for some soul revival than the Word of God! God wants us to understand that when we search in His Word, we will find comfort and joy. So be revived, be made wise, and receive joy and comfort as you dig into God's Word and let it work in you.

Teacher Tips

You could write the Old Testament books using one color marker and the New Testament books in a different color. Scramble the order of the books. For example, do not write Genesis, the first book of the Old Testament, and Matthew, the first book of the New Testament, on the same bag.

The more times the bricks are used, the more the bags will begin to loose their shape, making it increasingly difficult to build a wall. If the task of stacking used bricks becomes too frustrating, try extending the brick-laying line to 12 bricks long. This way the bricks will only need to be stacked three or four high.

Game Stats

- **Group size:** Small group or large group
- **Activity level:** 2
- **Space needed:** Classroom space

Warm Up

Make a masking tape line where each team is to build their wall. Make the line approximately eight brick lengths long.

To make bricks, turn the bags sideways. Write an Old Testament name on one side of the bag and a New Testament name on the opposite side of the same bag. Be sure the name is written on the front and back sides close to the bottom of the sack.

You will be making the bags into bricks by stuffing the bags with pieces of newspaper. Fold the end of the bag under one inch and tape the end closed.

You may choose to make a set of bricks for each team. Or use only one set of bricks and give each team an opportunity to be timed to see how quickly their team can build the wall. Once you have made the bricks, put the bricks into a large garbage bag for easy storage.

Gear List

- Brown paper lunch sacks (39 per team)
- Marker
- Newspaper (one sheet per lunch sack)
- Masking tape
- A large 33-gallon garbage bag for each set of bricks
- Timer (Optional)

Application

At the middle school age, many youngsters are bombarded with temptations to find comfort and joy in meaningless things. Sometimes these are addictive, harmful, or just wasteful of their time and resources. But they never satisfy for long. Help your students learn the books of the Bible through this fast-paced construction game. Together they help each other build a foundation using the books of the Bible where they can ultimately find comfort and joy in God's Word.

Goal of Game

Teams will try to build a brick wall in the order of the books of the Bible, either the Old Testament or the New Testament. The team that builds their wall first in the correct order wins. The wall must be standing when the last brick is laid.

Full Tilt

Place the trash bag containing the bricks about 20 feet away from the building line. You may either leave the bricks in the bag or make a pile of bricks. **The Israelite people found comfort and joy in God's Word. We can find comfort and joy in God's Word too. In this game you'll learn the books of the Bible. Every book of the Bible contains words that you can build your life on and that give comfort and joy. As a team you're going to help each other build a wall out of the books of the Bible.**

Point to the bag or pile of bricks. **In this bag/pile are bricks which have the books of the Bible written on them.** Point to the building line. **This is the building line. As a team you'll carry bricks from the bag to the building line. Players can only carry one brick at a time. Your team will build the wall by placing the bricks in the order of the books of the Bible, on the line. The team that finishes first with their books in the right order wins.** Be sure to tell the team if they are building the Old or New Testament. **When I shout, "Build on God's Word," you may begin.**

For two or more teams, use two sets of bricks. Mix the bricks together. Have two different building lines, one for each team. The team that builds their wall first wins. A brick that is dropped must be returned the starting pile.

Options: You might wish to add other elements to the game. Play the game in silence. Play the game with only one or two people who can "lay" the bricks on the wall. Play the game where bricks must be carried with a partner.

Finish Line

- **How did God's Word bring the Israelites comfort and joy? How does God's Word bring us comfort and joy?** *(The Israelites really listened and let God use His words to change them. They believed what God said and felt at peace because of it. We can be sure that God will do what He says, and that gives us comfort and joy, etc.)*

- **Tell about a time when you needed God's comfort and joy.** *(Answers will vary.)*

- **What's the difference between listening to God's Word and really hearing it?** *(We can hear it and not really pay attention. It can just sound like nice ideas but we don't ask God to show us what it really means. Our attitude matters—if we have an attitude of really wanting God's Word to work in our lives, it can, but an attitude of not really caring or not believing won't result in positive changes, etc.)*

TRUST

Scripture Reference
Job 1:1-3, 18-22; 42:10-13

Memory Verse
To you, O Lord, I lift up my soul;
in you I trust, O my God.

Psalm 25:1-2a

Bible Background

Job was not an Israelite, yet he worshiped the Lord and was an upright person. He obeyed God's law, revered God, and refused to participate in evil. Job was the wealthiest person in his land. In a single day Job suffered the equivalent of two terrorist attacks, a wildfire, an earthquake, and a tornado. His family was demolished, his house wrecked, and all his livestock and possessions were wiped out. Job probably thought things couldn't get worse, and yet they did. Sores popped out all over his body. Job could have easily blamed God for this appalling series of events. Instead, his response was to trust God.

Imagine all your circumstances have changed for the worst—your closest relationships have fallen apart and all your material possessions are gone. When life hurts, do you, like the psalmist, "take refuge in the Lord" (Ps. 118:8)? Do you cry out to Him, wait patiently for Him, and make the Lord your trust?

Trusting God during difficult times is like allowing Him to lift you out of the slimy pit and set your feet on a rock. Like Job, there is nothing wrong with feeling the emotions of loss and grief, while still understanding that God is in control.

Today's youth often experience tremendous hurt. They are exposed to more danger and brokenness than someone their age should have to face. Most youth do not know who can be trusted. Teach your young adolescents that God is the rock, the firm place for us to stand when it feels like the quicksand of life is sucking us down a hole. Just like Job, we can put our trust in God even when our life's circumstances look bleak. In God we can TRUST!

Teacher Tips

If it's a windy day and you're playing outside, try a rubber ball instead of plastic. The wind will not carry the rubber ball as easily. Have the players roll the ball instead of throwing it to tag out other players.

In some cases if the person rolling the ball is too far away from other players, he or she may take five steps toward a player, spelling the word TRUST as each step is taken.

Game Stats

- **Group size:** Small or large groups
- **Activity level:** 3
- **Space needed:** Large open area or outside open area

Warm Up

Use masking tape if indoors to make a large 10-foot circle. *Optional:* Try spray chalk if playing outside.

Write one letter of the word TRUST on each index card. Have about 5 to 10 sets of T-R-U-S-T cards. Players will receive a letter of the word each time they're tagged by the ball.

Gear List

- Large plastic kick ball (at least 12" in diameter)
- Masking tape
- Index cards
- Dark marker

Application

Even though bad things do happen, we can still trust totally in God. In this game, when players are tagged, a "bad" thing happens and they will gain a letter. Eventually the bad thing turns to good, when they use the letters to build the word TRUST. The player that actually experiences the most "pain" wins the game by building TRUST.

Goal of the Game

Players attempt to stay out of the way of the ball, but if tagged, gain a letter in building the word TRUST. The first one to spell out TRUST wins.

Full Tilt

Have all the players stand around the circle as you lay out the rules. **It can be very hard to trust God when bad things happen. Remember how Job lost everything, his house, his livestock, his health, and his family? Do you think he could have blamed God for all those rotten things? He didn't. He decided to keep trusting God. In this game, you might get tagged, which is a "bad" thing. But in the end you will see that experiencing bad things can help you to build trust in God.**

Give each player a number to remember. Start the game by being the player in the middle. Explain that you'll toss the ball in the air and call out a number. The player whose number is called should catch the ball while everyone else (including the person who tossed it) scatters. If the ball is caught before it bounces, that player tosses it in the air again and calls out a different number. (Other players won't want to run too far away!) Keep going until the ball bounces.

Once the ball bounces, the person whose number was called grabs the ball and shouts, "Trust God." Everyone must freeze when they hear those words. Then the catcher rolls the ball at any player. If a player is tagged with the ball, the player who was tagged receives the first letter in the word TRUST and subsequent letters thereafter if tagged again. The player who can spell TRUST first wins.

Finish Line

- **Why would Job continue to trust God after all the terrible things that happened to him?** *(He believed God would help him and do what was right. He had faith in God. He didn't have anything else to lose, etc.)*

- **How can we trust God when life hurts?** *(Keep reading the Bible and deciding to believe that it's true. Pray and tell God what we're feeling and ask Him to show His help and power to us. Hang out with other Christians who have a strong faith, etc.)*

- **What can we tell a friend when his or her life doesn't seem fair?** *(God knows what's happening to you, and He will work it out if you keep believing in Him. Don't stop trusting in God, etc.)*

Send Me

Scripture Reference

Isaiah 6:1-8

Memory Verse

Holy, holy, holy is the LORD Almighty;
the whole earth is full of his glory.

Isaiah 6:3b

Bible Background

In this passage Isaiah finds himself in the very presence of God. He was both awed and terrified to face the Almighty and Holy One. Truly encountering God produces a sharp inner awareness and conviction of our unworthiness and our sin. To come to an understanding of who God is changed Isaiah. His life was never the same because of the experience he had with God.

When was the last time you stood in wonder at a sunset, a child's laughter, or your own personality? One of the unfortunate things that characterize many adults is the loss of this fascination, this wonder of the handiwork of God all around us. Take time to "wonder" about the everyday things that God uses in your life to express His beauty, His power, and His faithfulness.

God is awesome, glorious, and holy, and when you experience Him, it will change you forever. Nothing compares to God. Help your young teens to "see" who God is. Help them to understand His awesome greatness. When your youngsters truly see the picture of who God is, they too will never be the same. They will respond like Isaiah and willingly say, "Here I am, send me!"

Teacher Tips

When making the cards, you might wish to ask the young people for words they think describe God. Make a set of cards using the students' suggestions.

Game Stats

- **Group size:** Small or large group (at least 8 students required)
- **Activity level:** 2
- **Space needed:** Classroom

Warm Up

Use masking tape to outline the playing area. Make a 15-foot square. In the center of the square make a 2-foot circle.

Teams should have at least six players. For each team make a deck of 12 cards. Write the following words, one on each card: *Awesome, Glorious, Holy, Merciful, Personal, Righteous, Forgiving, Pure, Eternal, Faithful, Loving, Powerful.*

Place the cards face down in the center of the playing circle. If you have four teams playing, you will place 48 cards in the circle.

Gear List

- 12 index cards per team
- Pen or pencil
- Masking tape

Application

How do you describe our awesome God? This relay race challenges players to match words used to describe God. They will be repeating the phrase, "Here I am, send me," throughout the game.

Goal of the Game

Team members attempt to collect cards that describe characteristics of God. The first team to collect the complete set of 12 cards wins.

Full Tilt

Divide into teams. Have each team sit on one side of the square. **Nothing can compare with God. He is totally amazing and unique. As a team you are going to discover how amazing God is. Your team will work to collect 12 cards that describe God.**

The first person in line runs into the circle, grabs one card, and runs back to the team line. Do not look at the card until you have returned to your team line. Once back at the team line, look at the card. If your team does not have that card, the team keeps it.

The next player in line shouts, "Here I am, send me." The team responds by shouting, "Go." That player runs to the center and picks up a card and returns to the team line. The team looks at the card. If the team already has the card, the same player must return the card to the circle, placing it face down, and return to the team line without a card. The next player in line then shouts, "Here I am, send me." The team responds by shouting, "Go." Your team needs to gather 12 different cards. Play continues until the first team has collected all 12 cards.

Finish Line

- **List as many characteristics of God as you can.** *(Students can use the card descriptions as well as others; accept all that are accurate.)*

- **How was Isaiah changed by seeing and experiencing God?** *(He was dedicated to his job as a prophet. He told God he was willing to go where God wanted him to go. Isaiah realized how sinful he was and how awesome God was. He saw himself as he really was. He had a huge respect for God, etc.)*

- **Isaiah was never the same after he encountered God. What will your response to knowing God be?** *(Students may not be able or willing to respond at this point. Encourage them to think about this; offer to listen if they want to talk about what they're thinking about.)*

Signs Say "This Way"

Scripture Reference

Isaiah 61:1-2; Luke 4:16-20;
Acts 13:23, 26, 29-30, 38-39

Memory Verse

Faith comes from hearing the message,
and the message is heard through the word of Christ.

Romans 10:17

Bible Background

In Old Testament times, the Jews were waiting for God to send the Messiah. The Messiah was going to save the people and deliver them from all their problems. But how were God's people to know who was the Messiah? Through the Old Testament prophets, God gave specific signs that the people could look for that would indicate who the Messiah was; only the Messiah would be able to fulfill all of these signs.

These passages are examples of how the Bible points to Jesus as our Savior. Help your middle school students see that many Old Testament passages predicted the Messiah would come, suffer, die, and come back to life again—and Jesus fulfilled all these Scriptures. There were many signs that pointed His way.

Do you remember the first time you heard the Gospel of Jesus Christ? Do you remember the first time you read your Bible and could understand it? How did you feel? For most of us it is an "aha" moment, as if a lightbulb finally is turned on in our heads and our hearts.

Many of your middle schoolers are at a turning point in their faith. Lightbulbs are turning on, and they are finally beginning to understand the Bible and who Jesus Christ really is. This is an exciting time in their lives, and we get to be a part of it!

Teacher Tips

An alternate way to start the game is to have all the players take a spot on a paper plate on the playing field. Look for the paper plates that are still open. Then place the Jesus plate on top of one of the remaining open spots.

This game can have very different results. Sometimes it's over quickly and sometimes it seems to last forever. To change this game, you can make several different spinners, using different directions.

Game Stats

- **Group size:** Small groups of fewer than 20 players
- **Activity level:** 1
- **Space needed:** Classroom space or gym

Warm Up

To make the playing area, spread out 25 paper plates into five rows of five. Place the plates at least one foot away from each other. If you wish, you can tape the plates to the floor. On one plate write "JESUS."

Make a spinner using another plate. Use the marker to divide the spinner/plate into six equal pie-shaped sections. In each section, write one of the following directions: skip one any direction, diagonal one, up one, down one, left one, right one.

Draw and cut out an arrow from the index card. Punch a hole in the center of the arrow. Attach it with the metal brad to the center of the paper plate. Be sure the arrow spins freely on the paper plate.

Gear List

- 27 or more paper plates
- Index card
- Metal brad
- Hole punch
- Marker
- Masking tape

Application

Middle school teens are often led in many directions that don't necessarily point them in the right way. In this game, players will try to get directions that point them to Jesus.

Goal of the Game

The players will move from plate to plate based on the spinner's directions. Each player's goal is to reach the Jesus plate.

Full Tilt

Place the Jesus plate on top of one of the plates on the playing field; make sure all the players know where the Jesus plate is. Players will stand on any paper plate, except for the Jesus plate. All players will need to face the same direction throughout the game.

In the Bible, many signs predicted the coming and identity of the Messiah. The signs all pointed to Jesus. In our lives, others can sometimes point us in the wrong direction. In this game, you're hoping the signs will point you to Jesus.

Spin the spinner. Call out the "sign" the spinner landed on. Wait for players to move accordingly. If their move would take them off the game area, they will remain on that paper plate. Only two players can occupy a plate at a time. If a third player lands on a plate, that player is out. The player who follows all of the signs and lands on the Jesus plate is the winner.

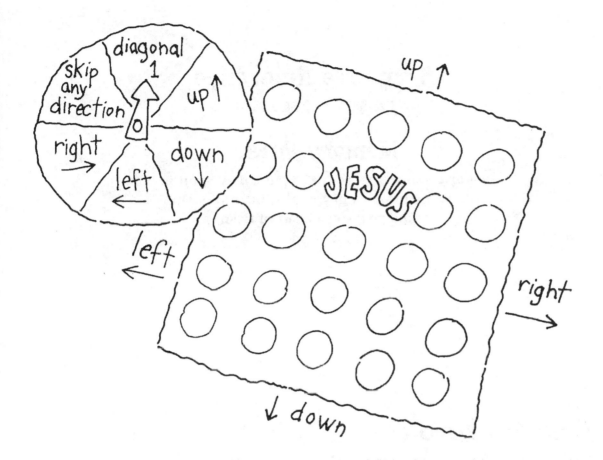

Finish Line

- **How do we know that Jesus was the Messiah?** *(The Bible tells us who He is. Prophecy said who He would be, and it all came true, etc.)*

- **In life, what points us in the right directions?** *(wise people, God, the Bible, good advice, etc.)*

- **Tell about a friend you know who needs to be pointed in the right direction. How will you help your friend?** *(Help them find good advice in the Bible. Get them connected with someone who is wise or knowledgeable. Help them think about all the possibilities, etc.)*

Heart Attack

Scripture Reference

Ezekiel 2:1-4; 36:24-28

Memory Verse

I will give you a new heart and put a new spirit in you;
I will remove from you your heart of stone
and give you a heart of flesh.

Ezekiel 36:26

Bible Background

There is at least one guarantee in life: change will occur. Over time people and places will go through a natural process of change. God is in the business of supernatural change. God can transform the hardest of hearts.

During Ezekiel's time, God's people had turned away from God, both in their actions and in their hearts. They worshiped idols and ignored God's laws. Their hearts had become like rock—cold, hard, and lifeless. The transformation of these hearts to again be in relationship with God required the touch of God's Spirit. Ezekiel witnessed the power of God's Spirit in changing the lives not only of individuals but of the nation.

Middle school students experience daily attacks on their hearts through the ungodly world around them, and the attacks of Satan on their spirits. Your middle schoolers need to know the Holy Spirit is still at work today. God cares and is involved in the daily struggles of His people. God can shine His light into the darkest of hearts. He has the power and the desire to transform your students' hearts. God is at work in their lives right now, and He has the power to help them become what He intends for them to be.

Teacher Tips

This is a game, but it is also a team challenge that requires players to problem solve.

Before starting, you can give each team three to five minutes to plan their strategy. Each team may solve this in a different way, which is all part of the game.

Game Stats

- **Group size:** Large group
- **Activity level:** 2
- **Space needed:** Large open space

Warm Up

Make masking tape starting and ending lines about 15 feet apart for each team. Place a box or basket at the ending line for each team. Cut out a red construction paper heart for each player.

Gear List

- Construction paper—one piece per player in 4 team colors, plus red for hearts
- Scissors
- Pens or markers
- Masking tape
- 4 baskets or boxes

Application

Middle school students will work together, offering to help their fellow teammates get their hearts safely to the basket. As they play, they can become more aware of the state of their own heart and their need for the Holy Spirit's renewal.

Goal of the Game

All the players on a team will try to get their hearts safely to the basket at the finish line. The first team to get all of their hearts safely in the basket wins.

Full Tilt

Divide into four teams. Have each team sit in a row behind their starting line. Give each team one color of construction paper so that each player has a piece. **This is your old heart of stone.** Team members use their hearts of stone to make a path across to the finish line, then students regroup and sit behind their starting lines. **We know God is in the business of changing hearts. He'll take our hearts of stone and make them hearts that are tender to His Spirit.**

Give each player a red heart. **This is your new heart.** Have players write their names on their hearts. **God wants each of us to keep our hearts sensitive to Him. He wants us to grow and change into the people He created us to be. He wants us to help and support each other in this journey of change. In this game, you'll help each other get your new hearts safely across the finish line. You'll see how together we can stand against attacks on our hearts as we carefully handle each other's hearts.**

Pick one team member to entrust your hearts to, then have everyone else go stand on your old stone heart. You must stay on your stone during the relay. When I say, "heart attack" the person you entrusted with your heart will pass it to the next person in the line and that person will pass it to the next until you get to the last person who will deposit your heart in the basket. The trick is that the hearts can only be passed using your elbows! To win, your team has to get all the team members' hearts into the basket. If you drop a heart while passing it, you must send it back to the beginning of the line. Begin the game.

start

end

Finish Line

- **Who can help us change our hearts?** *(Only God can do that.)*

- **What kind of change would you like the Holy Spirit to make in you?**
  *(Students will have various answers. Since this a very personal question,
  you may not hear many responses. Ask students to think about it and
  answer silently.)*

- **How can you be supportive or encourage your friends who might be
  struggling with attacks on their hearts?** *(Pray for them. Keep in touch
  with them. Check up on them and spend time with them. Make sure they're
  connecting with God.)*

Kneel Down

Scripture Reference

Daniel 6:3–5, 10–12, 16–17, 21–22, 26a

Memory Verse

Commit your way to the LORD;
trust in him and he will do this:
He will make your righteousness shine like the dawn,
the justice of your cause like the noonday sun.

Psalm 37:5–6

Bible Background

Daniel was one of the king's most valued advisors. Even as a young man, Daniel had been exceptionally talented and wise. In his later years, many were jealous of Daniel's position with the king. Everyone knew that Daniel was loyal to God and got down on his knees three times a day to pray to God. Jealous officials devised a law to forbid prayer to anyone but the king. This was their attempt to get rid of Daniel. Subsequently, Daniel was dropped into the lions' den for praying to God. Because of Daniel's obedience, God took care of him, sparing him from being eaten by the lions. Daniel obeyed God and trusted Him in the face of adversity.

Obeying God sounds pretty simple: just follow the directions, like putting together a model plane or baking bread. But obedience can bring hardships on us. When obedience starts to be costly, we start wavering. Sometimes our response is to make a show of obeying, but under the facade, we're avoiding the very thing God requires.

Thankfully, God forgives our confessed disobedience and gives us another opportunity. Obeying may be hard, but God will do wonders within us when we choose to obey. Help your young teens discover that God will take care of them through their obedience to Him. Obeying God doesn't mean life will be easy. Like Daniel, God will honor our right choices when we obey and trust Him.

Teacher Tips

Show an example of kneeling. Players must be completely kneeling to be safe. Caution players against saying they were kneeling when in fact they were not. If they're tagged while in the process of kneeling, they're out and must return to the beginning line.

To keep players from stalling and kneeling for long periods of time, you can periodically have a "jump up for joy" count. Count down from 10. At 0 everyone must "jump up for joy."

Game Stats

- **Group size:** Small or large group
- **Activity level:** 3
- **Space needed:** Large open space

Warm Up

Use masking tape to establish a beginning boundary line and an ending boundary line for the playing area.

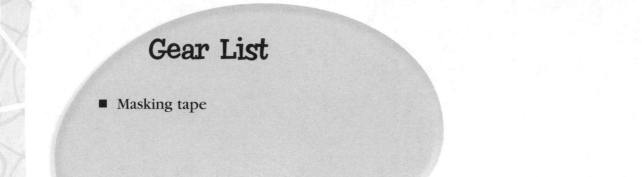

Gear List

- Masking tape

Application

Daniel was persecuted for praying three times a day. He was also saved because he was on his knees praying to God. In this game, players will be "safe" as long as they're on their knees.

Goal of the Game

Players will try to get from one end of the playing field to the other without getting "tagged" by lions. To keep from getting tagged, players kneel.

Full Tilt

Players stand at one end of the playing area. **Daniel was a man who obeyed God, even when the law said he couldn't. Daniel honored God by getting on his knees and praying three times a day. In this game, you're trying to get to the other side of the playing area.** Point out the designated area.

Choose four players to be lions; you need two lions per 10 players. Send these players to the middle of the playing area. **Lions, you must be on all fours; you cannot stand up.** Point to the four players. **These are lions. You want to stay away from them. If a lion tags you, you must return to the starting line.** (If a tagged player becomes too tired to start again, he can become a new lion, and the person he tags goes to the starting line in his place.)

But if you kneel down, you're safe and cannot be tagged. The first four people to reach the finish line become the new lions in the next game. Start the game. You can always change the number of lions in the center. The more lions, the more challenging it is for players to reach the finish line.

start

finish

Finish Line

- **Tell about a time when you have been in a situation in which you had to choose to obey God.** *(Students will have a variety of responses.)*

- **Tell about a time when it was hard for you to make a good choice when others were making a poor choice.** *(Students will have a variety of responses.)*

- **What can we expect from God when we obey Him?** *(to keep His promises to us, to help us when we need it, to hear us when we pray, etc.)*

Stand Alone

Scripture Reference

Amos 1:1; 7:10–17

Memory Verse

Blessed are you when people insult you, persecute you and falsely say all kinds of evil against you because of me. Rejoice and be glad, because great is your reward in heaven.

Matthew 5:11–12a

Bible Background

Amos was an ordinary person—a shepherd—sent by God to deliver a message of doom to the people of Israel because of their ungodly ways. Amos was probably laughed at and mocked because at the time, Israel was enjoying great prosperity and luxury. There was no sign of the pending calamity that Amos was predicting. Amos could have given up or changed God's message to make it sound nicer. He could have given in to the pressure of the people around him. But Amos, whose name means burden-bearer, took a stand for God. God gave Amos the strength to stand alone, and God will give us that same strength.

How can you prepare for those times when you feel you need to stand, but are afraid that you will have to stand alone? When you are standing for God, you are never really alone. He will always be there with you.

The middle school years are probably the toughest years in dealing with peer pressure. Standing alone is tough for your students because one of the greatest needs of a middle school kid is to be liked by others and to belong to a group. Sometimes taking a stand for God might mean that you have to leave the group.

Teacher Tips

If you're playing indoors, you can use tape to indicate the center area of the playing area instead of a box. This makes it easier for the players to grab the rewards.

Rewards can be anything: craft sticks are typically easy to find, or you can use balloons, sponges, bcanbags, or towels.

Game Stats

- **Group size:** Large group
- **Activity level:** 3
- **Space needed:** Large open space

Warm Up

Place one of the boxes in the center of the playing area.

Place the craft sticks in the center box. Space the other boxes 15 feet way from the center box.

Gear List

- 20 large craft sticks (or other identical items such as sponges, beanbags, towels, balloons)
- 5 boxes with no lids
- 4 different colored rolls of streamers
- Markers

Application

Hanging with the group in the game is much easier than having to stand alone. But standing alone is the only way to gain the rewards in this game.

Goal of the Game

Each team will try to get as many craft sticks as they can into their team boxes. The team with the most sticks at the end of the game wins.

Full Tilt

Divide into four teams. Have each team stand by their team box. Hand out the different colored streamers to each team. Team members will tie a piece of streamer to their upper left arms. If you wish, teams can label their boxes.

Then have the players on each team join hands in a line to form groups of three called gangs. While in their gangs, have the players decide who will be a head and who will be a tail. For each of the four teams, have two or three stand-alone players, not attached to any gang. Everyone will begin play behind his or her team's box. Then as the game is played, all players are free to go anywhere in the playing area.

In life, it's not easy to take a stand for God, especially if it means standing alone. In this game, those who are standing alone are the only ones who can get the rewards for your team. Have the stand-alone players raise their hands. **Each team player who's standing alone will be trying to get to the center box where the rewards are. You may only pick up one reward at a time and place it in your team's box. However, the gangs from the other teams are trying to stop you from standing alone. The gangs will try to capture you by encircling you.** Any stand-alone player who has a reward in his or her hand while encircled has to drop the reward where the tag occurred. Gangs cannot touch the rewards on the floor.

Have everyone who is a head raise his or her hand. **If the head of a gang tags a stand-alone player, that single player then becomes part of that gang as the new "tail." Gangs will become all mixed with players from different teams, and grow longer, which makes it harder to move, and that's part of the game. The team with the most rewards at the end of the game wins.**

Finish Line

- **At what times do you think you may need to stand apart?** *(at school, with a group of friends, in a club, in our families if they aren't Christians, when people are going against God's ways and we know we shouldn't go along with them, when someone insults God or other Christians and we know we should stand up for them, etc.)*

- **Why is it harder to be all by yourself than to be part of a gang?** *(We need to have friends. We have no support. We feel vulnerable and strange without someone to hang with. People pick on us or take advantage of us if we're alone, etc.)*

- **What do you risk when you are willing to stand alone for God?** *(getting labeled, losing our friends, being made fun of, getting beat up, being kicked out of somewhere we want to be, etc.)*

Get My Drift

Scripture Reference

Jonah 2:1-6; Matthew 12:38-41

Memory Verse

We must pay more careful attention,
therefore, to what we have heard,
so that we do not drift away.
Hebrews 2:1

Bible Background

We're all familiar with the story about Jonah's misadventures when he opted out of obeying God. Jonah's task as a prophet was to be a messenger—to take to the Assyrian capital of Nineveh the Lord's pronouncement that unless those Ninevites dramatically changed their ways and asked God's forgiveness, they'd be wiped out. Jonah was anything but keen on this job; the Assyrians were notoriously evil, and the arch enemies of his own people, the Israelites.

Jonah bailed out on the job, running the other direction. His journey was interrupted by a deadly ocean squall, landing him in the water when the sailors of the boat he was on finally took his advice and tossed him overboard. God's rescue vessel kept Jonah from drowning—a huge fish swallowed him and he passed an unimaginable three days inside the creature's digestive system before it belched Jonah onto dry land.

In responding to scribes and Pharisees who challenged Jesus for a sign of His deity, Jesus used the experience of Jonah to paint the picture of His upcoming death and resurrection. He told them that His resurrection would prove that He was the Messiah; He would come back to life just like Jonah returned to the land of the living after being in the fish's belly.

God certainly got Jonah's attention. Despite so much evidence of His identity, the Jewish leaders didn't get it—that Jesus was the Messiah they'd waited for. He didn't grab their attention the way they were anticipating. What captures your middle schoolers' attention? How often do they recognize God trying to catch their attention in the midst of their circumstances? Sometimes all that's needed is a reminder that God is there, waiting to be acknowledged. Move your preteens in that direction today.

Teacher Tips

Indoors may be better suited to this game since sound resonates better in an enclosed space.

If you have a reserved group, you might need to prod them to become worthwhile attention-grabbers.

Game Stats

- **Group size:** Large group
- **Activity level:** 2
- **Space needed:** Classroom space

Warm Up

Choose whether to use a maze or obstacle course; set it up, taking as much space as is available. Use natural obstacles, furniture, and items such as big boxes, traffic cones, preschool play equipment, a wide plank, etc. Leave room along the sides of the maze/course for students to occupy.

Give young people time to create attention-getting posters on half-sheets of poster board before the activity begins; they can use them during the game.

Lay out a basic course map with instructions for the partner to give to the student in the course. At specific places, the partner can say to do two push-ups, turn around three times, reverse course for 10 steps, turn left or right, crawl to the next obstacle, etc.

Gear List

- Noisemakers: bells, lids to clang together, horns, bullhorn, plastic jugs of pebbles or rice, kazoos, noisemakers
- Attention grabbers: flashlights, brightly colored streamers or flags
- Poster board cut in half
- Markers
- Stopwatch

Application

Many sights, sounds, and activities snag young people's attention. Are they looking for God in their everyday lives? This game prompts them to be on the lookout for God, who is trying to get their attention.

Goal of the Game

Players will try to navigate a maze or obstacle course while besieged by all types of sights and sounds. They will need to focus on their partner, who is trying to get their attention, to be able to complete the course.

Full Tilt

Choose several students and assign each a partner. The rest of the group will be attention grabbers.

Our lives are so full of activities, noise, media, and distractions; God has lots of competition for our attention. This maze/course will make us aware of how hard it can be for God to get our attention.

The students chosen will try to navigate the course one at a time, each trying to reach the end in the shortest time. Each one's partner will try to get their attention to give them directions on how to complete the course. The partner giving directions must speak in a normal voice and without dramatic gestures. Everyone else will do their best to distract and get the attention of the student following the course. They'll wave signs, flags, and streamers; make noise; turn flashlights on and off; sing; chant; and use other means to draw attention to themselves. Time each student who navigates the course.

Finish Line

- **What kinds of things pull your attention away from God?** *(friends, family issues, school, video games, sports, computers, music, being tired, being stressed, etc.)*

- **How does God get our attention?** *(He speaks to us when we're listening to the Bible being taught, responds to our prayers, uses other people to remind us He's there, lets difficult things happen to make us remember Him, gets us alone so we can listen, etc.)*

- **How can we learn to focus on God when we need to or when He is trying to get our attention?** *(Make time every day to pray and read the Bible. Be in church or a Bible study to learn God's Word every week. Learn to listen to Him so we recognize when He's speaking to us. Leave some quiet time or free time so God can get our attention. See how He got the attention of people in the Bible so we know what to look for, etc.)*

Mercy Me

Scripture Reference

Micah 1:1; 2:1–2; 6:6–8

Memory Verse

He has showed you, O man, what is good.
And what does the LORD require of you?
To act justly and to love mercy
and to walk humbly with your God.

Micah 6:8

Bible Background

The people in Micah's day behaved in harsh, self-absorbed ways. Now God was going to bring great punishment upon the people for their sins. Micah was pleading with the people to leave their evil ways behind and cling to God's ways. The people responded by offering a bribe to God of bigger and better sacrifices. That is not what God wanted. The outward show was not what He was after. He didn't want people just going through the motions.

All our Christian activities, like going to church, reading the Bible, singing in the choir, can be good. But sometimes, even the best of activities feels more like an obligation than a joy. Sometimes we simply go through the motions too. But God doesn't want empty actions; He wants a relationship with us.

Sometimes the relationship your youth have with the Lord is purely a ritual as well. Meanwhile, day in and day out, these youngsters deal with unfair treatment from other classmates, ridicule, put-downs, and bullies. Is it any wonder that today's kids don't understand what it means to act justly, love mercy, and walk humbly with Him? Indeed, do we?

Teacher Tips

After you play awhile, the tails may need to be replaced. Make extra tails for each team in case tails get accidentally torn or tattered.

Some players like to find ways to make it hard to take away their tails. Warn players against tucking in their tails too much. Be sure all tails stick out about the same length. Players can't loop their tails around belt loops or any other part of their clothing.

Other items useful for tails: socks, napkins, ribbons, paper towels, strips of newspaper, or strips of rags.

Game Stats

- **Group size:** Small or large group
- **Activity level:** 3
- **Space needed:** Large open space

Warm Up

You will need a large playing area. You might wish to cut the streamers into 2-foot lengths, one per player.

Gear List

- Rolls of different colored streamers for each team
- Scissors
- One long white sock per team

Application

Middle school youngsters rarely experience getting or giving mercy to others. Many disputes are focused on getting even or retaliation. In this game, youngsters have the opportunity to ask for and extend mercy to each other.

Goal of the Game

Players are able to extend mercy to one another when one's tail is removed; the team with the most players on the playing field after time has expired wins the game.

Full Tilt

Divide the teams so that there are at least four players per team. Each team needs a different colored streamer or "tail." Have players secure one end of their tails under their waistbands on their backs. Choose one player from each team to be the "mercy giver." These players have white socks for tails. **In this game, you're trying to grab the tails of the other team members. When you grab a tail you may toss it in the air and let it fall to the floor. You cannot crumple it up, step on it or kick a tail that's on the floor.**

If your tail is taken you must immediately sit down. You may not touch your tail even if it's within reach. You can call out for help by shouting, "mercy me." Only your team's mercy giver with the white sock tail can retrieve your tail. Once he or she retrieves your tail you may tuck it back in and play again because you have been granted mercy.

No one can take a mercy giver's tail except for another mercy giver. Once your mercy giver is out of play because his or her tail was taken, you will not receive any more mercy. The team with the most players with tails at the end of the game wins.

You might wish to stop the game after a designated amount of time. Alternately, a winner can be decided by the team that does not lose its mercy giver. As the game advances and there are fewer players you might wish to limit the playing space to a smaller designated area. Depending on the level and age of your players, you might wish to add a safe zone for each team. This would be a space where team members are safe from getting their tails removed.

Finish Line

- **How did it feel to be granted mercy?** *(good, safe, a relief, weird, etc.)*

- **When are times that you could show mercy to others?** *(when someone needs a place to stay or needs help, when someone has no food and you could share with them, when someone is sick or hurt, when you see a person who has less than you, etc.)*

- **What does God want from His people and from you?** *(to be fair with everyone, to show mercy, to obey Him, to do what's right, etc.)*

All in the Family

Scripture Reference
Luke 10:38–42; John 1:35–42; Romans 12:10

Memory Verse
Be devoted to one another in brotherly love.
Honor one another above yourselves.

Romans 12:10

Bible Background

In these Scripture references we are given two very different pictures of family interactions. In the one example of Mary and Martha, the two sisters are very focused on doing the "right" thing. In fact it is their difference of focus that creates a family conflict. Emotions start flying and friction emerges when the focus is clearly in the wrong place.

The other example shows how focusing on Jesus draws family members together. Andrew and Peter shared, got along with each other, looked out for each other, and wanted the best for the other person because each was focused on Jesus. When we concentrate on Jesus, our families will get along much better. Encourage your middle schoolers to make Jesus the main focus in their own lives, as a means for promoting family harmony.

To get along with your family, focus on Jesus. Paul teaches us to be devoted to one another in brotherly love, honoring each other above ourselves. But perhaps "brotherly love" doesn't look anything like honor in our own families! Another way to think of Paul's advice is this: to get along with others, set your sights on Jesus. He is the goal. If not the common goal between yourself and another person, then Jesus is the goal to which you hope to lead that other person. How can you focus on Jesus as you try to get along with your brothers and sisters this week?

Teacher Tips

You can use loops of ½-inch nylon rope instead of hula hoops. Tie the ends of the rope together forming a loop with a 36" diameter. Another option is to cut an old garden hose to a length of 9½ feet and join the ends with a 6" dowel.

This game is loads of fun to watch. Groups will be bumping into each other as they all try to touch the picture of Jesus. Be sure to designate someone to help families who fall over in their hula hoops. Use duct tape to repair hula hoops that come apart.

You can make the word "Jesus" more elaborate by using a word processing program and printing it out in a cool, colorful font.

Game Stats

- **Group size:** Any size
- **Activity level:** 2
- **Space needed:** Classroom

Warm Up

Make a masking tape start line for each team.

Tape the word "Jesus" on the wall opposite the starting lines.

Place a hula hoop at each starting line.

Gear List

- The word "Jesus" on a piece of paper
- 1 hula hoop per team
- Masking tape
- Duct tape (optional)
- ½-inch nylon rope (optional)

Application

With our fast paced society, together time for families has become less and less of a daily experience for young teens. This game is a race to see which family can come together the quickest by focusing on Jesus.

Goal of the Game

Teams that gather their family in the hula hoop first and return to the starting line are the winners.

Full Tilt

Divide the group into teams of six players. Direct each team to line up, one behind the other, behind a starting line.

Your team represents a family of six people. The first person in line will get into the hula hoop and run toward the word "Jesus." Remember that families who focus on Jesus get along. The person in the hula hoop will touch the word "Jesus" and run back to the team.

Once back at the start line the next person in line will join the first player inside the hula hoop and together they will run to Jesus, touch the word and run back. Keep adding another player to your hoop until your family of six is squeezed into the hoop. The first team, to have "all in the family" back to the start line wins.

Finish Line

- **What helps families get along?** *(being considerate of each other, not being selfish, thinking of what they need instead of only yourself, working hard to get along, etc.)*

- **How can focusing on Jesus help our families?** *(Instead of just thinking of what we want or need, we care how others are feeling or what they need. We have something in common when we all focus on Jesus. We can forgive easier and trust better. Jesus gives us more understanding of each other so we can show more care and love. Jesus helps us learn how to love instead of arguing or fighting, etc.)*

- **How can we get our families to focus on Jesus more?** *(Pray together. Eat meals together and give thanks out loud for Jesus. Talk about the problems we have and talk about what Jesus would say to do about them. Watch movies together that help us live the way God says to live. Do a community project together as a way to serve God, etc.)*

Shout Out

Scripture Reference

Acts 13:2–5a, 14, 42–46

Memory Verse

But you will receive power
when the Holy Spirit comes on you;
and you will be my witnesses in Jerusalem,
and in all Judea and Samaria, and to the ends of the earth.

Acts 1:8

Bible Background

The early Christians were persecuted for their belief in Christ. Witnessing to others and spreading the Good News was a risky venture. It was not easy to speak out boldly for Jesus knowing that you could pay a severe penalty, or even die, for doing so. It was only through the power of the Holy Spirit that Paul could face the challenges before him.

It's not easy for most young teens to boldly proclaim their faith. Help them to see the Holy Spirit is real and powerful and with them today, just as the Holy Spirit was with Paul and Barnabas long ago. The challenges today's young people face are different from the challenges before Paul and Barnabas. The places the young teens may frequent differ from those frequented by Paul and Barnabas. But the power the Holy Spirit has for us is the same. Your students can tap into the power of the Holy Spirit to find the boldness to speak publicly about Jesus.

Teacher Tips

After playing several times, you might wish to substitute current-day, familiar places for the ancient places: home, school, and two other well-known local places. Or you could change the ancient places to family, friends, relatives, and neighbors.

If you're playing outside on a field, tape the posters to backs of four chairs. Spread the chairs out in four different directions. You can also use a tarp as the center circle representing the ends of the earth.

Game Stats

- **Group size:** Small or large group
- **Activity level:** 3
- **Space needed:** Large open area or outside playing area

Warm Up

On each piece of poster board print the names of these ancient places—Antioch, Jerusalem, Judea, and Samaria. Tape one paper to each of the four walls around the room.

Make a masking tape circle 10 feet in diameter in the middle of the playing area. If playing outside, use rope to make the center circle.

Gear List

- 4 sheets of poster board
- Marker
- Masking tape
- 4 chairs (optional, if playing outside)
- rope (optional, if playing outside)

Application

Middle school students are generally not comfortable sharing their faith. This game will provide them the opportunity to "travel to ancient places" as they proclaim the Good News.

Goal of the Game

The players will be running to locations you'll call out. The last player to arrive at each destination is out. The goal is to remain in the game until it ends, with two or three players left.

Full Tilt

Paul and Barnabas took off on a mission trip to carry the Good News of Jesus to people in faraway places. Point to the locations. **The Holy Spirit told them to go to Antioch, Jerusalem, Judea, and Samaria. And they went to the ends of the earth as they knew it.**

Point to the center circle. **This circle represents the ends of the earth. When I say, "Spread the Good News," I'll give you a location. You are to run to that location and proclaim, "Jesus is the Christ, the Son of God." If I say, "the ends of the earth," everyone must sit in the circle and proclaim the Good News. The last person to arrive at each location is out.**

Point out a designated area where the players who are out can hang out. Start play by shouting out a location. After the kids have arrived at that location, send the last player to arrive out of the game. Continue this process until only two or three players are left. They win. To make the game more challenging, as you call out the location, point the players in the wrong direction.

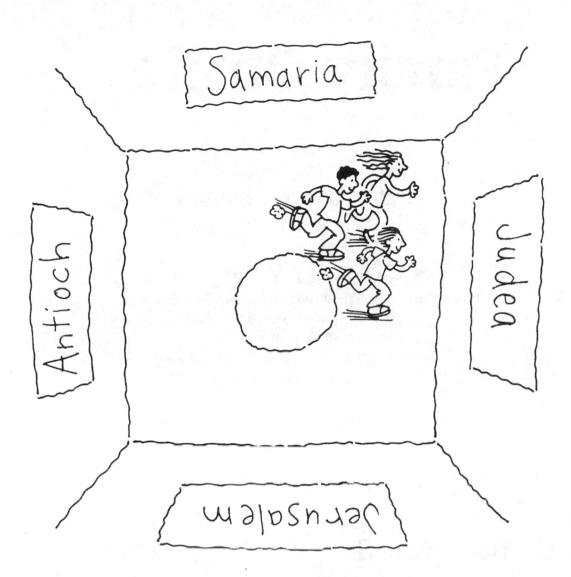

Finish Line

- **Paul and Barnabas's missionary trip wasn't a game. How did they keep going?** *(They had each other for encouragement. They let the Holy Spirit show them where to go and who to talk to. They trusted God to cause people to listen; etc.)*

- **What can help you speak boldly about what you believe?** *(knowing what I believe well enough to explain it to someone else, praying for courage, having a Christian friend with me, practicing with other Christians first, believing that the Holy Spirit is going to help me, etc.)*

- **Who is one person you believe the Holy Spirit is giving you an opportunity or desire to tell about Jesus?** *(Give students a chance to share openly.)*

Family Circle

Scripture Reference

Acts 13:16–17, 21–23, 26, 38–39; Galatians 4:4–6

Memory Verse

But when the time had fully come, God sent his Son,
born of a woman, born under law,
to redeem those under law,
that we might receive the full rights of sons.

Galatians 4:4–5a

Bible Background

The Jews were God's chosen people. They had been waiting hundreds of years for a Messiah to deliver the Jewish people from enemies and oppressors. Jesus came to earth to be the Messiah, the Savior. But God's message of redeeming love embodied in Jesus was not meant for the Jews alone.

God sent His Son to offer forgiveness of the sins of the world that extended beyond the Jews. Through Jesus, any person who believes in His power to forgive will be freed from the law and redeemed. Paul proclaimed this Good News to everyone, both Jews and Greeks.

But also remember that you, too, have been born of God. As Christians, we have all the rights and privileges of children of God. We have God's favor and His never-ending love. Celebrate your own birth as a child of God! Let your middle school students see this week the hope and joy you have as one of God's children.

Teacher Tips

Players have to be in close proximity to each other during this game. Be sure to monitor play closely. Emphasize safety and appropriate touch.

Once players grab hold of the player's hands across from them, they cannot let go. If the group begins to fall and players release each other's hands, the group must start over. Players may change their grip, but they cannot totally let go.

Game Stats

- **Group size:** Small or large group
- **Activity level:** 2
- **Space needed:** Classroom

Warm Up

Play this game as one large group or divide into teams of 7-14 players. If using teams, the teams will compete against each other.

The team that finishes first by forming a circle from the tangled arms wins. If there is only one team, you can keep track how long it takes the team to get into the family circle.

Gear List

■ None

Application

Middle school students rarely look at each other as members of the same family. Our belief in Jesus makes us children of God; therefore we are all in His family. This game produces the picture of forming a family circle.

Goal of the Game

Once having joined hands with other players in a circle, students try to untangle the giant knot that they've created without letting go of each other's hands. The goal is to undo the tangled knot and restore the circle—without breaking their connection.

Full Tilt

You will need an even number of players for this game. If you have an odd number, make one player your assistant.

Paul had a tremendous challenge in delivering the Good News of Jesus, the Messiah, to both the Jews and the Greeks. Two groups of people from very different lifestyles were brought together by their belief in Jesus. We're all from different walks of life too. The message Paul delivered is still true for us. Our belief in Jesus makes us children of God, one big family. Let's play a game where we make one big family circle.

Have players join hands to form a large circle, then they can drop hands. Have the group take several steps in to form a tight circle, then they'll reach out with one hand and grab hold of the hand of a player across from them. It cannot be the hand of the player directly next to them. Then have the players reach their other hand across and grab hold of someone else's hand.

Now you have all come from different walks of life. Let's see if you can work together without letting go of your hands to form one big family circle. Players will try to untangle the knot they've made. Hands must always remain grasped together. If hands do accidentally come apart, start the game over again. Once the group has successfully finished their challenge, have them shout out, "We are part of God's family circle."

Finish Line

- **Why did God send His only Son?** *(to save us, to give us eternal life, to make us part of His family, etc.)*

- **What does it mean for us in everyday terms that we're all part of God's family?** *(We need to show we care about each other. We all have the same thing—Jesus—in common. We all are forgiven the same way. Being part of the same family means we keep connected to each other and value each other because of Jesus, etc.)*

- **How can we know for sure that we're part of God's family?** *(If we've asked Jesus to forgive us for what we've done wrong and choose to live His way, we can be sure we have a place in God's family. The Holy Spirit lives in us, etc.)*

Second Chance

Scripture Reference

Acts 12:25; 13:4–5, 13; 15:36–41; 2 Timothy 4:11

Memory Verse

Be kind and compassionate to one another,
forgiving each other, just as in Christ God forgave you.

Ephesians 4:32

Bible Background

In the 2 Timothy reference, Paul gave us an example about forgiveness and giving others a second chance. There had been a strained relationship between Paul and Mark. In fact Mark left Paul during a missionary journey. Paul felt that Mark had deserted him.

After time passed, Paul forgave Mark and gave him a second chance; then Paul includes Mark on another missionary journey. Our God is a God of second chances. God has given us a second chance, one that we do not deserve.

Young teens are involved and consumed with being best friends or worst enemies and often that's with the same person. Their relationships are not stable; one day they stand up for their friends and the next they are tearing them apart.

Middle schoolers are typically concerned about who likes who, who did what to whom, and what they think about different people. They often bear grudges and plot revenge against those who have hurt them or who have appeared to hurt them. It's not uncommon that little time is spent on mending relationships, let alone giving others a second chance. Challenge your youngsters to extend a second chance to others, even when they feel someone does not deserve it.

Teacher Tips

Safety first! Be sure all players understand that tosses must be below the shoulders. Outlaw shots toward the head. If someone hits another player in the head, that player is permanently out of the game.

You could also play this game outdoors and add a little splash to it. You could use soccer cones to mark the dividing line on the playing field. Replace the balls with sponges. You'll need a bucket of water on each side of the playing area. Sponges fly much further when soaked in water. Begin the game with 10 sponges and one bucket on each side of the playing field.

Game Stats

- **Group size:** Small or large group
- **Activity level:** 3
- **Space needed:** Large open space

Warm Up

Divide the playing area in half. Use the tape to mark a center line. Place the 10 balls on the center line.

Gear List

- 10 small soft foam balls
- Masking tape
- Sponges and buckets (optional, for outdoor play)

Application

Rarely do middle school youngsters experience getting or giving a second chance. In this game players will have a partner who grants them a second chance to get back into the game.

Goal of the Game

Players attempt to get opposing team members out by throwing a ball at them. There is no team winner; instead whenever a player is out, they're given second chance to get back into the game.

Full Tilt

Giving others a second chance is not an easy thing to do. Paul knew this and set an example for us to follow. Paul forgave his friend Mark and gave him a second chance. In this game, you will get some practice in giving others a second chance.

Divide into two teams. Each team will stand on one side of the playing area. Have the players find a partner on their own team. Direct one of the partners to stand in the playing area while the other partner stands on the sideline.

When I shout, "second chance" players in the playing area run to the center line to retrieve a ball. Players cannot cross their team's line and must stay on their own side at all times. Players may only throw the balls underhanded—no overhand throwing. If a player hits you with a ball or catches the ball you've thrown, you're out. When you are out, you go to your sideline. Say to your partner, "you get a second chance." Then your partner goes into the game. When your partner is out, he or she will give you a second chance and you can return to playing the game. You are either playing or waiting along the sideline for your second chance.

After playing for a while, have the teammates switch partners. Or have everyone on the sidelines switch teams and then find new partners on their new team.

Finish Line

- **How did this game show what it means to give a second chance to a friend or family member?** *(We give or get a second chance even when it's not deserved. It's about being willing to give a second chance, and not about what the person deserves or earns. We can make someone's day by giving a second chance. It makes a difference if we do it. We need to think how we would feel if we needed the second chance, etc.)*

- **How does if feel to be able to give someone else a second chance to play?** *(Answers will vary.)*

- **What can you do to fix broken relationships?** *(Give someone another chance to be my friend. Remember that I will need a second chance too. Be willing to let go of the past and try again. Learn how to forgive. See things from the other person's side, etc.)*

Dig In

Scripture Reference

Acts 17:10–12; 2 Timothy 2:15

Memory Verse

The unfolding of your words gives light;
it gives understanding to the simple.

Psalm 119:130

Bible Background

We learn from Paul, the Bereans, and Timothy that reading the Scriptures is one way to get to know God better. Getting to know God requires time and effort the same way as getting to know people better. Just as the Bereans studied to know the truth, we need to be diligent in studying Scripture so that we can really know God. Show your students that digging into the Bible is not just a history lesson; it's reading a living, breathing love letter to us from God.

Reading and studying are hardly passions of most preteens. In fact for most students at this age the words "reading" or "studying" bring instant images of schoolwork. However many of these same students are often caught writing notes or text messaging each other during class. What is the difference? In class they have to or are made to do the work that doesn't seem to apply to their lives or interests. Writing notes, emailing, and text messaging are young people's way of getting to know someone or gaining information regarding someone else. They have a desire to know and that takes the sting out of the process. Try to open up a new window of understanding about what digging into the Bible can be about, and that it's the one best way to know God.

Teacher Tips

You can make additional sets of any Bible verse or write the books of the Bible on the packing peanuts. Really make them dig for the truth!

The tendency in this game is for the teams to end up having peanuts everywhere. If this happens, make it a condition for winning that all the peanuts without verses written on them are picked up before declaring a winner.

Game Stats

- **Group size:** Any
- **Activity level:** 3
- **Space needed:** Classroom

Warm Up

One large box of packing peanuts will work for a group of about 8.

Pull 14 packing peanuts from the large box. Write each word from the Bible verse, including the reference, on one of each of the 14 peanuts. (The unfolding of your words gives light; it gives understanding to the simple. Psalm 119:130).

Toss the peanuts back into the box and mix well. You can use one box for all the teams and time the teams. Or you can make a box with the verse on the peanuts for each team.

Gear List

- A large box for each team
- A large amount of packing peanuts for each team
- Fine-tipped permanent marker
- Stopwatch (optional)

Application

History doesn't top the thrill list for most middle schoolers. Put a little excitement into digging into His story, the Bible, by giving teens a fun opportunity to literally dig for God's Word.

Goal of the Game

Teams race to dig in, find, and put in order the packing peanuts with the words from the Bible memory verse on them.

Full Tilt

If using one box, have the other teams wait as you time one team. The team that completes the task in the least amount of time is the winner. If using more than one box, the teams can race to see which team completes the task first. Place the box, or boxes, in the center of the playing area.

Digging into God's Word can be fun and exciting especially when you learn cool things about God. In this game, your team is going to have fun as you dig in and find a Bible verse. Each word of the verse is written on a packing peanut. Be the first team to find all pieces to the Bible verse and put them together in proper order and you win.

Before you begin, have the teams stand about five feet away from their box. Teams may run to their boxes when you start play by stating: "Dig in!"

Finish Line

- **What difference does it make how well you know God?** *(If I don't try to get to know Him, I won't understand what the Bible means or what God wants for me. Having a close relationship with God means trying to get to know Him better all the time, etc.)*

- **How does knowing God's Word help you to know God better?** *(I know what He thinks is important. I find out how to talk to God and how to hear Him talking to me. I learn how to grow in my faith. I see how God works, etc.)*

- **What one thing do you think you can do now to get more into the Bible and know God better?** *(Students will suggest a variety of ideas such as reading the Bible first thing in the morning, having a devotional time, listening in church. Try to have them make their ideas personal, specific, and measurable rather than general and vague.)*

Lend a Helping Hose

Scripture Reference
Acts 18:24-28

Memory Verse
Therefore let us leave the elementary teachings about Christ and go on to maturity.

Hebrews 6:1

Bible Background

Christian maturity is not a matter of being the smartest Bible scholar, getting old, or attaining a high position in the church. Growing in Christ is about accepting help from others, gaining more understanding, and responding to God's Word with your heart. Apollos was a very wise and learned man. He had all the head knowledge of God's Word that was available at the time.

When he met Aquila [ACK-wih-luh] and Priscilla, Apollos could have easily disregarded their comments and teachings, because he was much smarter than they. But Apollos listened to them and learned a great deal. His heart was changed. Because of the help Apollos received from Aquila and Priscilla, he was able to preach and teach the Gospel in ways that strengthened the faith of others.

Information alone will not move your adolescents to grow in Christ. The youngsters in your care need to see the value in how we can help each other by responding with our hearts toward each other. Together we can support each other, show acts of kindness toward each other, and extend grace to each other. We all could use a helping hand to help us grow as Christians.

Teacher Tips

To make this game more challenging have players keep both ends of the hose touching at all times. You could also make it a requirement that all players stand on one leg.

There are times as you lead groups of young teens that you sense turmoil brewing within the group. Perhaps kids are bickering or the group is having a tough time with one particular preteen. This activity could be used time and time again to help the group focus on what's needed to help each other grow in Christ. You might say, "I sense we need a helping hose." Then break out the garden hose activity.

Game Stats

- **Group size:** Small or large group
- **Activity level:** 2
- **Space needed:** Classroom

Warm Up

Clear an area in the classroom. Be sure the garden hose has been well drained and is at room temperature so it will be flexible.

Gear List

■ A 10-foot length of rope or garden hose for each team

Application

Middle school students will have the opportunity to help each other and work as a team as they concentrate on growing spiritual characteristics.

Goal of the Game

The players will cooperatively create simple pictures using a garden hose. The speediest team with the most creativity wins.

Full Tilt

Apollos was one smart man when it came to knowing the Scriptures. You could say his spiritual garden had been planted, but nothing was growing until he met Aquila and Priscilla. Because of their help his spiritual garden began to grow. How does your spiritual garden grow? Together we can help each other learn more and grow deeper in our walk with Christ. In this game, you'll work with others by lending a helping hose!

Have the players grab the hose with both hands—the more players the more fun. If you have more than 20 players, try breaking into more than two teams with a hose for each team. The teams can then race each other.

Begin the game by shouting out a word, such as *heart, tent, Bible, cross, flower* (show it growing), *sun,* and *cup.* These are all words found in the Scripture that correspond to this theme of this lesson. You can ask the players for other words that would fit this activity.

Players work together using the hose to make a picture of that word. They must keep both hands on the hose and cannot let go of the hose at any time. The first team to create the item's image wins. You might wish to add points for creativity too. You can use extra young people or youth workers as judges for the creative aspect of each creation.

Finish Line

- **Who has helped you to grow as a Christian?** *(Responses will vary. Ask those who respond to be specific about how the person they named helped them.)*

- **How can we help each other to grow as Christians?** *(Be accountable to someone for our growth. Challenge a friend to memorize verses with us. Read the same book separately and talk about it regularly. Pray for each other. Be willing to have a friend show us or tell us when we're blowing it. Keep each other responsible for coming to church. Ask our friend what he's learning spiritually or how he's doing with his relationship with God. Accept others the way they are and believe in them, etc.)*

- **Explain how you have grown as a Christian in the past year.** *(Responses will vary. After this question, you might spend some time praising God for the ways various group members have grown.)*

Soul Mates

Scripture Reference

Acts 20:16–25, 36–38

Memory Verse

By this all men will know that you are my disciples,
if you love one another.

John 13:35

Bible Background

In this passage, Paul is setting a standard and defining what a true and "good" friend ought to be. One of the true measures of a friend is seen during the rough and tough times we go through. Paul was about to face prison and persecution. Paul and his friends showed true qualities of a great friendship despite their looming circumstances. They were supportive, trustworthy, and loyal. They put serving others as their top priority and did not let their own needs interfere with the best interests of their friends. Paul and his friends had a great friendship because they put Jesus first.

Friendships mean different things to us in different stages of our lives. Along the way friends might be called playmates, best friends, kindred spirits, buddies. It usually isn't until we're older and wiser that our friendships deepen to become more than people we hang out with or tell our secrets to. Somewhere we come to a turning point when we recognize that serving and sacrificing are crucial aspects of our friendships.

Friends are typically the highest priority in the life of a middle school youngster. The word *friend* can take on many meanings to people. Not all friends are the same, and not all friendships are the best kind. Prompt your young teens to discover that the best friendships and relationships are those that put Jesus first. Jesus loves each and every one of us deeper than we can ever imagine. It is in Jesus that we can find our true soul mate.

Teacher Tips

To avoid injuries, forewarn players that when they approach the pile of shoes, they need to keep their eyes forward and their heads up. This may reduce the likelihood of players bonking their heads. Prohibit players from diving into the pile of shoes.

Another way to play this game is to deliver a shoe to each player from the pile. Have the players put on the one shoe. The challenge is to find the matching shoe. It may be in the pile or on someone's foot.

Game Stats

- **Group size:** Small to large group
- **Activity level:** 2
- **Space needed:** Classroom or outside

Warm Up

You'll need a large space free from obstacles.

Gear List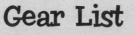

- None

Application

Adolescents seek love, acceptance, and belonging in friendships. In this game, youngsters look for their "sole" mates and share with each other the qualities of good friendships.

Goal of the Game

Players will try to locate their shoes in a chaotic pile of footwear.

Full Tilt

Jesus wants you to be content and have the best kinds of friends. Finding a true friend or a soul mate who puts Jesus first will make you truly happy. Let's play a game where you'll find your sole mate.

Have players sit in a large circle and take off both shoes. Designate several players to collect the shoes and pile them up in the center of the circle. Then jumble the pile to mix up the shoes.

Begin the first round of play by giving students a signal to run to the pile and find a pair of matching shoes that are not their own. They must put on that pair of shoes and go back to sit in the circle.

At your next signal, kids will have to find the person wearing their shoes. To reclaim their own pair of footwear, each player must tell the other a quality of a good friend. Then they'll put their shoes back on and sit down. (You could also have them thank each other for being a friend.)

You can play again, having students find any two shoes, matching or not, then locating the owners of both and sharing different friendship qualities. Once they all have their shoes back, have them call out the qualities they heard shared. Conclude by explaining that our best soul mate is found in our own relationship with Jesus. Jesus is our best friend and foundation upon which we should build our friendships with others.

Finish Line

- **Define the qualities of a good friend.** *(trustworthy, fun, keeps a secret, is honest with me, doesn't turn on me, likes me no matter how I act or look, etc.)*

- **What difference have you seen it make in a relationship that does put Jesus first?** *(People get along better. There's not as much competition. We don't get into fights. We have more patience and trust. We don't have to try to be someone we're not, etc.)*

- **How do you go about trying to put Jesus first in a friendship?** *(Talk about it. Get involved in doing projects that are based on serving Jesus. Ask God to give me ideas. Look at other people who do it, etc.)*

Goody Two-Shoes

Scripture Reference

Acts 22:3-4; Philippians 3:4-9

Memory Verse

This righteousness from God comes
through faith in Jesus Christ to all who believe.
There is no difference, for all have sinned
and fall short of the glory of God.

Romans 3:22-23

Bible Background

In trying to show the Jews that personal merit alone is insufficient to please God's righteous nature, Paul had an impressive list of recommendations. Rather than boasting about his achievements in the Philippians passage, Paul used his background to show the religious Jews that all we count as "gain" is still inadequate to God.

Paul understood that all his attempts to follow the religious law and do all the right things were never enough to please God. The only way to find favor with God was to trust in Christ to forgive him. No matter how moral or good we are, no matter how many righteous things we've accomplished, when compared to Christ and His righteousness, our best can never be good enough.

Many young people consider themselves religious because of the things they do. They might attend church and youth group or be in involved in a Bible study. Many times youngsters equate salvation with these religious acts. Middle schoolers need to hear Paul's message: no matter how good or religious we are, these acts are never enough to earn God's favor. Not one is good enough or can do enough to get into heaven. Our best efforts or actions are not what saves us. Salvation can only be found in Jesus. Being good is just not good enough—we have to have Jesus.

Teacher Tips

Have small brown paper bags or zip-top bags available for youngsters who might be wearing flip-flops or other shoes that do not allow for easy cotton ball gathering.

Game Stats

- **Group size:** Small or large group
- **Activity level:** 2
- **Space needed:** Classroom

Warm Up

Use the masking tape to make a large circle. The circle needs to be at least 15 feet across. For large groups make the circle as big as the space allows.

Gear List

- A small bag of cotton balls
- Large bag of packing peanuts
- Masking tape

Application

We want students to understand that doing good things and living as a Christian are essential for demonstrating our faith and love toward God. Help them to recognize however, that these things cannot save them or earn their entry into heaven. In this game, middle schoolers will discover that despite their attempt to gather as many "good" things as possible, it just won't be good enough without Jesus.

Goal of the Game

Players all pair up with a partner. Each player takes off one shoe (and sock if necessary) to use as a "goodie gatherer" for the cotton balls and packing peanuts the pair picks up with their toes. The packing peanuts represent good efforts we pack into our lives. The cotton balls represent God's grace. Once all the cotton balls and packing peanuts have been collected, the partners will discover that only the cotton balls which represent God's gift of grace count. The team with the most cotton balls wins.

Full Tilt

Have all the players find a partner and stand with their partner on the circle line. **Many people are confused about what it means to be a Christian. Many think that if you are a really good person, a Goody Two-Shoes, you will go to heaven. Let's think of good things people do to try to get into heaven.**

As young people shout out answers, spread the cotton balls and packing peanuts within the circle. **Everyone take off one shoe and sock. When I say, "Goody Two-Shoes," you and your partner will begin to use your toes to collect as many cotton balls and packing peanuts as possible. Stash them in your two empty shoes. When all the "goodies" have been collected, find your partner and stand along the outside of the circle.**

Now count to see how many you collected. Allow time for students to count total items collected. **Now recount only the cotton balls.** Wait for their reaction; then explain.

The packing peanuts represent all the good efforts that we can pack into our lives, which are not good enough to get us into heaven. The cotton balls stand for God's grace. So those are the only ones you can count for this game. It is because of God's grace that we are saved, not because of the good things we do.

Finish Line

- **Name some things people do which they think will save them or earn their way into heaven.** *(go to church, help the poor, give offerings and tithes, be nice to people, share, etc.)*

- **How would you explain the idea of grace to someone who is trying to live a good life to please God?** *(Students will have various responses. Aim toward this definition: undeserved favor.)*

- **Why is it harder to depend on God's grace than to try to do good things to reach heaven?** *(We don't deserve God's favor so we try to work hard. Being good seems more real than accepting grace. What if grace doesn't work after all but you didn't do all the right things—then what will happen to you?)*

Blessing Brigade

Scripture Reference
Acts 28:16–23; Philippians 1:12–14

Memory Verse
"For I know the plans I have for you," declares the LORD,
"plans to prosper you and not to harm you,
plans to give you hope and a future."
Jeremiah 29:11

Bible Background

In this passage, Paul was arrested in Jerusalem by the Romans. This could have been viewed as a tragedy. How could this happen to someone who was doing so much good for others by spreading the Word of God? Paul could have stopped everything he was doing for God in order to "save" himself. But God used Paul's arrest as an opportunity to spread the Gospel. God took the "bad" stuff that was happening in Paul's life and turned it into "good" stuff.

Often when bad things happen to us, we can become depressed, feel powerless, and want to give up. We do not have the benefit of seeing how tragedy, loss, and pain will affect our lives a month or a year from now. That's God's advantage. All we're asked to do is trust and obey Him. If we choose not to believe that God does indeed cause *all things* to eventually work for good, then we invite the bad stuff of life to create a bitter spirit, which chokes the peace of God in our hearts.

Paul's experience should be an encouragement to us all. God has the power and the ability to turn bad into good. Help your young teens begin to trust God. God can take the bad and ugly circumstances in their lives and turn them into great opportunities full of blessings for themselves and others.

Teacher Tips

As players pull on the hula hoop, the hoop tends to come apart. Have duct tape or a couple of back-up hula hoops available in case of breakage. Alternately, you could use a 9½ foot length of ½" plastic or nylon rope. Tie the ends of the rope together to form a loop 36" in diameter.

Before you start the game, designate which player inside the hula hoop will be the first to be free and which one will remain. Once play begins be sure that players are rotating turns inside the hula hoop.

Game Stats

- **Group size:** Small or large group
- **Activity level:** 3
- **Space needed:** Large open space or outside playing area

Warm Up

You will need a large space for players to run from one end of the playing area to the other.

Gear List

- 2 hula hoops
- Duct tape for hoop repair
- Nylon rope (optional)

Application

In this game, players can be tagged out, which is a "bad" thing. Then a group of players, the Blessing Brigade, can bless the person who is out, allowing the player to return to the game again, which is a "good" thing.

Goal of the Game

Players try to avoid being tagged as they run from one end of the playing field to the other. If they do get tagged, they're frozen, which is "bad." The other players within hula hoops are the Blessing Brigades. If a Blessing Brigade encircles a frozen player, that player is then blessed and eventually unfrozen, which is "good."

Full Tilt

Paul was in prison and this was a "bad" thing. Yet God took Paul's "bad" circumstance and turned it into "good." Have the players stand along one side of the playing field. Choose two players to be Roman guards. Put the two players in the center of the playing field. Point to the Roman guards. **These are Roman guards.**

When I shout, "Blessing Brigade" all the rest of you will run to the other side of the playing field and wait there. Point to the other side of the playing field. Be sure the players know where the ends of the playing field are. **As you run, you want to stay away from the guards. If a guard tags you, you must freeze where you are.**

Choose two players. Have each player get inside one of the hula hoops. Place these players in the center of the playing field. Point to the players in the hula hoops. **These players are the Blessing Brigades. If you're frozen, they will come to bless you. When you're blessed, you will become a new Blessing Brigade member. You get into the hula hoop and the other player will now go free. The new player now becomes the new Blessing Brigade. The players inside the hula hoop will be continually changing.**

Start the game by calling out "Blessing Brigade." Players run from one side of the playing area to the other and wait there. Then you will call out again for the group to run back to the original start line. Continue to call out "Blessing Brigade" to signal players to run back and forth. For more excitement you can add more guards or more Blessing Brigades.

Frozen Player

Blessing Brigade

Guard

Finish Line

- **How does God turn "bad" things into "good" or blessings?** *(He can use the hard things we went through to help us grow up or learn something. We can be of help to someone else who is going through the hard thing we already went through. The bad thing can end up putting us in a new place or situation that's better than where we were before, etc.)*

- **How are the struggles you face like being frozen in the game?** *(Bad things make us want to hide or pull away. When a bad thing happens, we feel like our life is on hold or ending, etc.)*

- **What can you do when it seems like a lot of bad things are piling up in your life?** *(Ask God to help me reach out to my friends for support. Keep waiting for the good things to come out of the bad ones. Don't give up, etc.)*

Clique Together

Scripture Reference
Ephesians 2:12–22

Memory Verse
You are no longer foreigners and aliens,
but fellow citizens with God's people
and members of God's household.

Ephesians 2:19

Bible Background

Christ is the barrier breaker between alienated and hostile groups of people. This passage deals with two groups of people who believed in Jesus as the Christ—Jewish Christians and Gentile Christians. Historically, these two groups had been completely separated. Jews were God's chosen people. The Jewish religion had been very exclusionary. The Jews were given the blessings, promises, and privileges of God. The Gentiles were considered aliens and outcast.

Paul spoke of Christ breaking down this barrier. Because of Christ those who were once alienated from God are now considered to be members of God's household. Because of what Christ did on the cross, racial, gender, and class differences do not affect our relationship with Christ. Paul gave a vivid description of the Church as a body whose parts are all different yet work together. But when one part works against the rest of that body, it can do serious harm to the work at hand.

As members of Christ's household we are to submit ourselves to one another in reverence for Him. There are no excuses for not submitting, for not trying to get along, or for not honoring one another. We love because He first loved us. We submit to one another because this is a demonstration of submitting to our Lord and Savior. Therefore we should love one another and worship God together in unity. Impress on your students that Jesus loves everyone. It is wrong to isolate others. We should all clique together.

Teacher Tips

Use a couple of players to demonstrate a "good" tag and "bad" tag. Good tags are gentle and below the waist. *Options:* Instead of streamers you could use craft sticks or sheets of paper towels.

Game Stats

- **Group size:** Small to large group
- **Activity level:** 2
- **Space needed:** Open classroom space

Warm Up

Use masking tape to make a large 16-foot circle. Divide the circle in half using another strip of tape. Use small pieces of tape to mark tick lines on the large circle about a foot apart. (If you have 16 or more players, mark 16 lines, 8 on each side of the circle. If you have less than 16 players, make a mark for each player, dividing them on each half of the playing area.) Use the marker to number each line on each side of the playing field half circle. Each side will have the numbers 1 through 8.

Make a smaller 2-foot circle in the center of the large circle. Cut the streamers into 1-foot lengths. Each time you play the game you will need 3 streamers. Cut as many pieces of streamer as needed to play as many times as you wish. Place three streamers inside the small circle, laid across the dividing line.

Cut the lids off of the boxes. Place one box, outside each side of the large circle.

Gear List
- 2 rolls of streamers
- 2 empty boxes
- Masking tape
- Permanent marker

Application

Middle schoolers often form exclusive groups based on many factors. In this game, players will form different groups that intermingle with each other. As they play, they learn that everyone can "clique together" making them all winners.

Goal of the Game

Each player will stand on a number on the large circle line. The leader will call out different numbers. The players whose numbers are called try to pick up streamers and place them in their team box without getting tagged by any of the other team.

Full Tilt

Have the players stand on a numbered line around the circle. Extra players enter the circle on space numbered 1 on one side of the circle. Players leave the playing area from the other side of the playing area from the highest numbered space.

We all belong to a number of different groups of people. Groups you belong to may include classes at school, your family, school sports or activity groups, and church groups. But sometimes when we are in small groups, or cliques, we tend to treat others differently. Perhaps we put them down or make them feel as though they don't fit into "our group." Jesus wants us to include everyone. In this game, you will discover that we all belong to different groups, but that those groups can truly clique together. When I call out a number or group of numbers, players on those numbers will rush into the center and pick up a streamer. You can only pick up one streamer at a time. Try to put your streamer in your team's box without getting tagged by players from the other side of the circle whose numbers were also called.

You will call out pairs or groups of numbers. For example shout, "1 and 3 clique together." OR "even numbers clique together." The players whose numbers were just called run to the center of the circle and grab a streamer. They are trying to put the streamers into their team's box. Players from opposite sides of the circle are trying to tag each other out. If a player who has a streamer gets tagged, their streamer does not get added to the team's box, but instead the streamer gets returned to the center for the next round of play.

For the next round of play have all the players return to their numbered spots. Then say, "everyone clique together." Have the entire group rotate one spot clockwise. If you have extra players, one player enters on the number one spot on one side of the playing area, while one player exits the playing area from the highest numbered spot on the other side of the playing area. Players will now have a different number and may also be playing for the other team now. Play at least 16 times. At the end of play, count the streamers in each box. Then ask everyone who had been on the winning team to raise their hand. Every hand should go up. Everyone will have been different numbers on different teams and played with different players. Everyone will have cliqued together and everyone will be a winner.

Finish Line

- **Why does Jesus want us to include everyone?** *(He includes everyone in salvation and we need to follow His example. Every person has the same value to God no matter what they look or act like. Including everyone shows non-Christians something about Jesus, etc.)*

- **How can you include others in your normal activities, making them feel comfortable, like teammates?** *(Ask them to join us. Eat lunch with them or hang out where they do. Invite them to our house or to church. Share music or other common interests with them.)*

- **Describe a time when others left you out. How did it make you feel?** *(Accept responses, acknowledging feelings and vulnerability.)*

Topic Index

Scripture Index

Full Tilt: Wacky Games

Title	Page	Scripture Reference	David C Cook LifeLinks to God New Life College Press Reformation Press Wesley Anglican	Echoes The Cross
Hey, Obey!	14	1 Samuel 15:1–3, 7–15, 20–22, 24–26, 28–29	Unit 25 Lesson 2	Unit 25 Lesson 2
Cool Covenant	18	2 Samuel 7:8–17; Hebrews 8:10–13	Unit 25 Lesson 4	Unit 25 Lesson 4
Hang Out	22	1 Kings 11:1–10	Unit 26 Lesson 6	Unit 26 Lesson 6
Winner's Circle	26	1 Kings 16:29–31; 18:17–24, 36–40	Unit 26 Lesson 8	Unit 26 Lesson 8
Clean It Out	30	2 Kings 17:6–8, 11b–14, 16–18, 22–23; 2 Chronicles 36:11–12, 14–17a, 20	Unit 27 Lesson 10	Unit 27 Lesson 10
Books of the Bible Battle	34	Nehemiah 8:1–12	Unit 27 Lesson 12	Unit 27 Lesson 12
Goody Two-Shoes	98	Acts 22:3–4; Philippians 3:4–9	Unit 28 Lesson 1	Unit 28 Lesson 1
Family Circle	78	Acts 13:16–17, 21–23, 26, 38–39; Galatians 4:4–6	Unit 28 Lesson 3	Unit 28 Lesson 3
Shout Out	74	Acts 13:2–5a, 14, 42–46	Unit 29 Lesson 5	Unit 29 Lesson 5
Soul Mates	94	Acts 20:16–25, 36–38	Unit 29 Lesson 7	Unit 29 Lesson 7
Blessing Brigade	102	Acts 28:16–23, Philippians 1:12–14	Unit 29 Lesson 9	Unit 29 Lesson 9
Lend a Helping Hose	90	Acts 18:24–28	Unit 30 Lesson 11	Unit 30 Lesson 11
Second Chance	82	Acts 12:25; 13:4–5, 13; 15:36–41; 2 Timothy 4:11	Unit 30 Lesson 13	Unit 30 Lesson 13
Send Me	42	Isaiah 6:1–8	Unit 31 Lesson 2	Unit 31 Lesson 2
Mercy Me	66	Micah 1:1; 2:1–2, 6:6–8	Unit 31 Lesson 4	Unit 31 Lesson 4
Get My Drift	62	Jonah 2:1–6; Matthew 12:38–41	Unit 32 Lesson 6	Unit 32 Lesson 6
Stand Alone	58	Amos 1:1; 7:10–17	Unit 32 Lesson 8	Unit 32 Lesson 8
Heart Attack	50	Ezekiel 2:1–4; 36:24–28	Unit 33 Lesson 10	Unit 33 Lesson 10
Kneel Down	54	Daniel 6:3–5, 10–12, 16–17, 21–22, 26a	Unit 33 Lesson 12	Unit 33 Lesson 12
Dig In	86	Acts 17:10–12; 2 Timothy 2:15	Unit 34 Lesson 1	Unit 34 Lesson 1
Treasure Hunt	10	Joshua 1:8; Psalms 1:2; 119:11, 15, 47, 97, 165; 1 Timothy 4:15	Unit 34 Lesson 3	Unit 34 Lesson 3
TRUST	38	Job 1:1–3, 18–22; 42:10–13	Unit 34 Lesson 5	Unit 34 Lesson 5
All in the Family	70	Luke 10:38–42; John 1:35–42; Romans 12:10	Unit 35 Lesson 7	Unit 35 Lesson 7
Fill Your House	6	Deuteronomy 6:6–9, 20–21, 24	Unit 35 Lesson 9	Unit 35 Lesson 9
Clique Together	106	Ephesians 2:12–22	Unit 36 Lesson 11	Unit 36 Lesson 11
Signs Say "This Way"	46	Isaiah 61:1–2; Luke 4:16–20; Acts 13:23, 26, 29–30, 38–39	Unit 36 Lesson 13	Unit 36 Lesson 13